# Prayer Poems

# PRAYER POEMS

Compiled by

O. V. *and* Helen Armstrong

Granger Index Reprint Series

BOOKS FOR LIBRARIES PRESS
FREEPORT, NEW YORK

Copyright © 1942 Whitmore & Stone
Reprinted 1969 by arrangement
with Abingdon Press

STANDARD BOOK NUMBER:
8369-6094-7

LIBRARY OF CONGRESS CATALOG CARD NUMBER:
72-86793

MANUFACTURED
BY
HALLMARK LITHOGRAPHERS, INC.
IN THE U.S.A.

# Foreword

Turn these pages reverently,
  For here are hearts at prayer:
"Where two or three or joined," Christ says
    He will be there.

Among this throng of worshipers
  If one but look to see,
There is a Presence—keep quite still
    For it is He.

—GRACE NOLL CROWELL

# Contents

## From Day to Day

## The Festal Days

## The Small Circle

## The Large Circle

## Discipleship

## The Soul's Needs

## SUPPLEMENT
### Poems About Prayer

## Acknowledgments and Indexes

# From Day to Day

MORNING

EVENING

MIDNIGHT

# From Day to Day

## MORNING

*And in the morning, rising up a great while before day, he went out, and departed into a solitary place, and there prayed.*

—Mark 1:35

### MORNING PRAYER

O God, who comest with the dawn,
    With light and love and cheer,
Grant me to know with burning heart
    That Thou art always near.
Shine on the way in which I walk,
    Upon the folk I meet;
And grant that friendliness and joy
    May make each day complete.

—CALVIN W. LAUFER

### PRAYER

Lord, the newness of this day
Calls me to an untried way:
Let me gladly take the road,
Give me strength to bear my load,
Thou my guide and helper be—
I will travel through with Thee.

—HENRY VAN DYKE

*My voice shalt thou hear in the morning, O Lord; in the morning will I direct my prayer unto thee, and will look up.* —Ps. 5:3

## UNTO THEE

Not for the eyes of men
   May this day's work be done,
But unto Thee, O God,
   That, with the setting sun,
My heart may know the matchless prize
Of sure approval in Thine eyes.

—THOMAS CURTIS CLARK

## MATINS

These things I do engage to do;
Hourly to keep my doing true
   To what my conscience knows;

To send my soul upon its round
Of this day's duty with no sound
   Of plaining of my woes;

To live more worthy of their love
Whom I do love all else above—
   And fight my rightful foes.

God give me guidance in my ways
   To do the things I should;
God give me length and strength of days
   To do the things I would.

—JOHN FINLEY

## WHEN I AWAKE, I AM STILL WITH THEE

Still, still with thee, when purple morning breaketh,
   When the bird waketh and the shadows flee;

*Let the words of my mouth, and the meditation of my heart, be acceptable in thy sight, O Lord, my strength and my redeemer.*

—Ps. 19:14

Fairer than morning, lovelier than the daylight,
   Dawns the sweet consciousness, I am with thee.

Alone with thee, amid the mystic shadows,
   The solemn hush of nature newly born;
Alone with thee in breathless adoration,
   In the calm dew and freshness of the morn.

Still, still with thee; as to each new-born morning
   A fresh and solemn splendor still is given,
So doth this blessed consciousness, awakening,
   Breathe, each day, nearness unto thee and heaven.

When sinks the soul, subdued by toil, to slumber,
   Its closing eye looks up to thee in prayer;
Sweet the repose beneath thy wings o'ershading,
   But sweeter still to wake and find thee there.

So shall it be at last, in that bright morning,
   When the soul waketh, and life's shadows flee:
O in that hour, fairer than daylight dawning,
   Shall rise the glorious thought, I am with thee.
              —HARRIET BEECHER STOWE

## JUST FOR TO-DAY

Lord, for to-morrow and its needs,
   I do not pray:
Keep me, my God, from stain of sin,
   Just for to-day;
Let me no wrong or idle word
   Unthinking say:
Set Thou a seal upon my lips,
   Just for to-day.

*But exhort one another daily, while it is called To day.*—Heb. 3:13

Let me both diligently work,
    And duly pray;
Let me be kind in word and deed,
    Just for to-day;
Let me in season, Lord, be grave,
    In season, gay;
Let me be faithful to Thy grace,
    Just for to-day.

In pain and sorrow's cleansing fires,
    Brief be my stay;
Oh, bid me if to-day I die,
    Come home to-day;
So, for to-morrow and its needs,
    I do not pray;
But keep me, guide me, love me, Lord,
    Just for to-day.

        —SYBIL F. PARTRIDGE

# EVENING

*And at even, when the sun did set, they brought unto him all that were diseased. . . . . And he healed many.*

        —Mark 1:32, 34

The day Thou gavest, Lord, is ended,
  The darkness falls at Thy behest;
To Thee our morning hymns ascended,
  Thy praise shall hallow now our rest.

        —JOHN ELLERTON

## EVENING PRAYER

God of Mercy:
  The day with all its choices, good or ill,
  Is now beyond recall;

*Evening, and morning, and at noon, will I pray, and cry aloud; and he shall hear my voice.*    —Ps. 55:17

And I am alone with Thee,
To make answer for deed and word and thought.
I cannot play the hypocrite with Thee;
I cannot excuse or justify the blots that stained the day;
I cannot lightly laugh at my transgressions now;
For Thou dost know me altogether.
But Thou dost know the good in me, and not the evil only;
Dost see my struggles, mark my resolutions,
Hear my silent prayers in heaven, Thy dwelling place.
Thy heart is kind.
There is forgiveness with Thee.
It was for men like me that Jesus died.
For His sake, let me know Thy peace tonight,
And with the morrow make me to be
A new and worthier man.

—ROBERT FREEMAN

## VESPER BELLS

The days are filled with duties;
Each moment has its care:
But evening bids us worship
And kneel in humble prayer.

The vesper bells now softly
Caress the fading day;
Their silver tones are pleading
With men to kneel and pray.

—DWIGHT EDWARDS MARVIN

## PRAYER AT THE CLOSE OF A MARRED DAY

Take unto Thyself, O Father,
This folded day of Thine,
This weary day of mine;

*Let my prayer be set forth before thee as incense, and the lifting up of my hands as the evening sacrifice.* —Ps. 141:2

15

Its ragged corners cut me yet,
O, still the jar and fret!
Father, do not forget
    That I am tired
  With this day of Thine.

Breathe Thy pure breath, watching Father,
  On this marred day of Thine,
  This erring day of mine!
Wash it white of stain and spot!
O, cleanse its every blot!
Reproachful Eyes! remember not
    That I have grieved Thee
  On this day of Thine!
      —ELIZABETH STUART PHELPS

## FROM DAWN TO EVENSONG

From dawn to evensong is but a day;
The hours so swiftly pass away,
And yet I would not have them stay,
  For night brings home and rest.

Be this my prayer, when evening shadows fall,
To him whose love o'ershadows all;
"In every trial, great and small—
  "Dear Lord! I've done my best."

With loved ones gathered safely at my side,
Beyond the stress of time and tide,
Come, Lord, and with us all abide,
  Be thou our honored Guest.
      —C. AUSTIN MILES

*But it shall come to pass, that at evening time it shall be light.*
      —Zech. 14:7

## EVENING

O Lord, the sun is low;
　With me abide;
Dark shadows 'neath their wings
　Bring eventide.

Thy presence, Lord, was mine
　The livelong day;
I welcome night, for Thou
　Hast heard me pray.

—ROBERT J. CRAIG

## TONIGHT

For all who watch tonight—by land or sea or air—
O Father, may they know that Thou art with them there.

For all who weep tonight, the hearts that cannot rest,
Reveal Thy love, that wondrous love which gave for us Thy best.

For all who wake tonight, love's tender watch to keep,
Watcher Divine, Thyself draw nigh, Thou who dost never sleep.

For all who fear tonight, whate'er the dread may be,
We ask for them the perfect peace of hearts that rest in Thee.

Our own belov'd tonight, O Father, keep, and where
Our love and succor cannot reach, now bless them through our
　prayer.

And all who pray tonight, Thy wrestling hosts, O Lord,
Make weakness strong, let them prevail according to Thy word.

—AUTHOR UNKNOWN

*Yet the Lord will command his lovingkindness in the daytime, and in
the night his song shall be with me, and my prayer unto the God of
my life.* —Ps. 42:8

17

## PRAYER OF A TIRED WOMAN

Lord, when my bedtime comes tonight, I pray
Sleep shall blot out the problems of this day.

But, if through such Nirvana that should gleam
That flickering pattern of little dream,

Then, of Thy goodness, lead my lagging feet
Beside still waters in green pastures sweet.

Let me forget all care, so when at length
Dawn wakens me, I shall have gained new strength;

To gird my armor for another day,
And with fresh courage, get me on my way!
—MAZIE V. CARUTHERS

## BEDTIME PRAYER

Lord, Thou knowest how I live;
All I've done amiss forgive:
All of good I've tried to do,
Strengthen, bless, and carry through:
All I love in safety keep,
While in Thee I fall asleep.
—HENRY VAN DYKE

## VESPERS

Lord of the tender twilight sky,
The stars that march beneath Thine eye,
The years that roll unheeding by,
Hear Thou our evening prayer.

*Where is God my Maker, who giveth songs in the night?*
—Job 35:10.

Lord, Thou art wise and well dost know
What daunts Thy children here below,
How lives are spotted deep with woe
   And nights are black with care.

Lord, help us keep our faith in day
And hear Thine answer when we pray.
Help us to lift our hearts and say—
   Tomorrow will be fair.

—CLARIBEL WEEKS AVERY

## AN EVENING PRAYER

The day is ended.  Ere I sink to sleep,
  My weary spirit seeks repose in Thine.
Father, forgive my trespasses, and keep
  This little life of mine.

With loving-kindness curtain Thou my bed,
  And cool in rest my burning pilgrim-feet;
Thy pardon be the pillow for my head;
  So shall my sleep be sweet.

At peace with all the world, dear Lord, and Thee,
  No fears my soul's unwavering faith can shake;
All's well, whichever side the grave for me
  The morning light may break.

—HARRIET McEWEN KIMBALL

## EVENING PRAYER

Holy Father, bless us
As the day we close,

*I remember thee upon my bed, and meditate on thee in the night
watches.*    —Ps. 63:6

And the night's refreshing
　　Grant us in repose.

All the day Thy presence
　　Made our hearts to burn,
As we heard Thy counsel,
　　Felt Thy Love's concern.

So tonight we pray Thee
　　Leave us not alone;
But through light and shadow
　　Keep us as Thine own.

Grant to us in slumber
　　To be very near,
In Thy goodness quelling
　　Needless doubt and fear.

When at length the dawning
　　Sweeps the night away,
Help us rise triumphant,
　　Worthy of the day.

　　　　　　　—CALVIN W. LAUFER

## AN EVENING PRAYER

If I have wounded any soul today,
If I have caused one foot to go astray,
If I have walked in my own willful way,
　　Dear Lord, forgive!

If I have uttered idle words or vain,
If I have turned aside from want or pain,
Lest I myself shall suffer through the strain,
　　Dear Lord, forgive!

*Hear my cry, O God; attend unto my prayer.*　　　—Ps. 61:1

If I have been perverse, or hard, or cold,
If I have longed for shelter in Thy fold,
When Thou hast given me some fort to hold,
     Dear Lord, forgive!

Forgive the sins I have confessed to Thee;
Forgive the secret sins I do not see;
O guide me, love me, and my keeper be,
     Dear Lord, Amen.

          —C. MAUDE BATTERSBY

# MIDNIGHT

*I will both lay me down in peace, and sleep: for thou, Lord, only makest me dwell in safety.*

          —Ps. 4:8

## A PRAYER

Lord, when on my bed I lie,
Sleepless unto Thee I cry;
When my brain works overmuch,
Stay the wheels with Thy soft touch.
Just a quiet thought of Thee,
And of Thy sweet charity,
Just a little prayer, and then
I will turn to sleep again.

          —JOHN OXENHAM

## NIGHT-WATCH PRAYER

Lord, Thy peaceful gift restore,
Give my body sleep once more:
While I wait my soul will rest
Like a child upon Thy breast.

          —HENRY VAN DYKE

*He giveth his beloved sleep.*

          —Ps. 127:2

21

## SLEEPLESSNESS

Why is it that I cannot rest?
E'en though the sun within the west
Has long since left the cloudlands red,
I lie still tossing on my bed
   In troubled wakefulness.

Worries upon the night intrude
And fill me with solicitude,
While rampant thoughts run to and fro
Like whirlwind storms of sleet and snow
   With ceaseless restlessness.

Then memories of laden days
In which I trod earth's lonely ways
Lead me to think about my cares,
My business and my home affairs,
   And bring me deep distress.

Speak to me, Lord, and calm my mind,
My wayward thoughts in thralldom bind.
Beneath me put thine arms, I pray,
And to my troubled spirit say,
   "Let me thy soul possess."

             —DWIGHT EDWARDS MARVIN

# The Festal Days

NEW YEAR

EASTER

THANKSGIVING

CHRISTMAS

# The Festal Days

## NEW YEAR

*So teach us to number our days, that we may apply our hearts
unto wisdom.*

—Ps. 90:12

### PRAYER FOR THE NEW YEAR

> Day by day,
> Dear Lord, of Thee three things I pray:
> To see Thee more clearly,
> Love Thee more dearly,
> Follow Thee more nearly,
> Day by day.
>
> —RICHARD OF CHICHESTER

### ANOTHER YEAR IS DAWNING

> Another year is dawning!
>   Dear Master, let it be,
> In working or in waiting,
>   Another year with Thee.
> Another year in leaning
>   Upon Thy loving breast,
> Of ever-deepening trustfulness,
>   Of quiet, happy rest.

*This one thing I do, forgetting those things which are behind, and
reaching forth unto those things which are before, I press toward the
mark.* —Phil. 3:13, 14

Another year of mercies,
　Of faithfulness and grace;
Another year of gladness,
　In the shining of Thy face.
Another year of progress,
　Another year of praise;
Another year of proving
　Thy presence "all the days."

Another year of service,
　Of witness for Thy love;
Another year of training
　For holier works above.
Another year is dawning!
　Dear Master, let it be
On earth, or else in heaven,
　Another year for Thee!
　　　　　　　—FRANCES RIDLEY HAVERGAL

## A PRAYER

Through every minute of this day,
　Be with me, Lord!
Through every day of all this week,
　Be with me, Lord!
Through every week of all this year,
　Be with me, Lord!

So shall the days and weeks and years
　Be threaded on a golden cord,
And all draw on with sweet accord
　Unto Thy fullness, Lord;
　That so, when time is past,
By grace I may at last
　Be with Thee, Lord!

　　　　　　　—JOHN OXENHAM
*Abide with us.*　　　　　　　—Luke 24:29

## CROWN THE YEAR

Crown the year with Thy goodness, Lord!
  And make every hour a gem
  In living diadem,
    That sparkles to Thy praise.

Crown the year with Thy grace, O Lord!
  Be Thy fresh anointing shed
  On Thy waiting servant's head,
    Who treads Thy royal ways.

Crown the year with Thy glory, Lord!
  Let the brightness and the glow
  Of its heavenly overflow
    Crown Thy beloved's days!
                    —Frances Ridley Havergal

## NEW YEAR PRAYER

As the Old Year seeks the shadows,
  That lie black beyond the hill,
Where the summer twilight listened
  To a plaintive whippoorwill,
My glad heart is softly praying,
  "Though I walk with joy or rue,
Let me have the strength to labor
  At what God would have me do!"

While the bells fling jubilations
  Through the reaches of the skies
In my heart a prayer is lifting,
  "Let me be both kind and wise,

*Let your light so shine before men, that they may see your good works,*
*and glorify your Father which is in heaven.*        —Matt. 5:16

27

As I give myself for others,
  As I lean to them and share
All the anguish and the burdens
  That their souls and flesh must bear!"

As the New Year comes with singing
  Through the wind-stripped orchard trees,
Where ripe apples spilled their fragrance,
  Lo, I do not ask for ease,
But my heart is humbly praying,
  "As I walk life's crowded way,
God, let each tomorrow find me
  More like Jesus than today!"

—EDGAR DANIEL KRAMER

## A LITTLE PRAYER

That I may not in blindness grope,
  But that I may with vision clear
Know when to speak a word of hope
  Or add a little wholesome cheer.

That tempered winds may softly blow
  Where little children, thinly clad,
Sit dreaming, when the flame is low,
  Of comforts they have never had.

That through the year which lies ahead
  No heart shall ache, no cheek be wet,
For any word that I have said
  Or profit I have tried to get.

—SAMUEL E. KISER

*And they took knowledge of them, that they had been with Jesus.*
*—Acts 4:13*

28

## THE NEW YEAR

Upon. the threshold of the year we stand,
Holding Thy Hand;
The year holds mysteries and vague surprise
To meet our eyes;
What will its passing moments bring,
To weep, or sing?

We fear to take one step without Thy care
And presence there;
But all is clear to Thine all-seeing gaze,
Counting the days
From dawn of time, till ages cease to be—
Eternity!

Upon the threshold of the year we stand,
Holding Thy Hand;
Thou wilt walk step by step along the way
With us each day;
So whether joy or woe shall come this year,
We shall not fear!

—HOMERA HOMER-DIXON

## A NEW YEAR PRAYER

If any little word of mine<br>
May make a life the brighter,<br>
If any little song of mine<br>
May make a heart the lighter,<br>
God help me speak the little word,<br>
And take my bit of singing,

*And be ye kind one to another.*  —Eph. 4:32

And drop it in some lonely vale
  To set the echoes ringing.

If any little love of mine
  May make a life the sweeter,
If any little care of mine
  May make a friend's the fleeter,
If any lift of mine may ease
  The burden of another,
God give me love and care and strength
  To help my toiling brother.

—AUTHOR UNKNOWN


## NEW YEAR'S MORNING

We humbly ask, dear Master,
  That our New Year gift may be,
All meaner things forsaking,
  Rich fellowship with Thee.
Our hearts at rest and tranquil,
  Thy blessed will our own
Until we know Thee fully
  In Thy eternal home.

—AUTHOR UNKNOWN


## PRAYER AT NEW YEAR'S

For bringing us this fair New Year,
  We lift our love and praise.
Go with us, Father, every mile,
  And bless us, all the days.

—NANCY BYRD TURNER

*I will therefore that men pray every where, lifting up holy hands.*
—I Tim. 2:8

## MY ONLY PLEA

Just one thing, O Master, I ask today,
Now that the old year has passed away
And a promising new year, through grace of Thine,
With all the dreams of youth is mine—
Just one thing I ask as I onward go,
That I'll walk with Thee—not too fast, nor slow;
Just one thing I ask and nothing more,
Not to linger behind, nor run before.
O Master! This is my only plea—
Take hold of my life and pilot me.

—WALTER J. KUHN

## NEW YEAR

Dear Master, for this coming year
    Just one request I bring:
I do not pray for happiness,
    Or any earthly thing—
I do not ask to understand
    The way Thou leadest me,
But this I ask: Teach me to do
    The thing that pleaseth Thee.

I want to know Thy guiding voice,
    To walk with Thee each day.
Dear Master, make me swift to hear
    And ready to obey.
And thus the year I now begin
    A happy year will be—
If I am seeking just to do
    The thing that pleaseth Thee.

—AUTHOR UNKNOWN

*He giveth power to the faint; and to them that have no might he increaseth strength.* —Isa. 40:29

## NEW YEAR

I thank Thee, God, for New Year's Day—
    The chance to turn a clean white sheet,
To fold past records all away,
    So failure-marred, so incomplete.

Grant me to make this year of mine
    A thing of beauty and of flame—
A poem strong and crystal-fine,
    And at the end to sign my name.

—MARIE BARTON

# EASTER

*Why seek ye the living among the dead?  He is not here, but is risen.*

—Luke 24:5, 6

## AN EASTER PRAYER

O Crucified Son of God, I pray
All hate and evil in me slay.
That I may live with spirit free
Not unto self, but unto Thee.

Risen, living, triumphant Lord,
Breathe in my soul Thy living word,
That risen, I may walk with Thee,
Within appointed paths for me.

Ascended now upon Thy throne
Thou wilt not leave us here alone.
Holy Spirit, walk by our side
And bless us on this Eastertide.

—CHESTER M. DAVIS

*Jesus said unto her, I am the resurrection, and the life.*
—John 11:25

# EASTER

I have an Easter house today;
The winter's grime is washed away,
My chairs and tables burnished bright,
My mirrors giving back the light;

And roses, fresh from nature's loom,
In springtime beauty and perfume,
Work miracles in every room.

Have I an Easter heart today?
No litter left, no cobwebs grey?
The corners swept so clean and bright
My Lord therein may find delight?

O Christ, new risen from the tomb,
Come, Rose of Sharon, fill each room
Of this poor heart with sweetest bloom!

—MARY HOGE WARDLAW

## EASTER PRAYER

In a sweet springtime,
   Half the world away,
Jesus Christ arose for us
   At the break of day.

Now again it's springtime—
   Bending low we pray:
Bless us, Lord of Easter,
   On Thy Easter Day!

—NANCY BYRD TURNER

*And they found the stone rolled away from the sepulchre.*
—Luke 24:2

## EASTER PRAYER

Oh, let me know
The power of Thy resurrection!
Oh, let me show
Thy risen life in clear reflection!
Oh, let me soar
Where Thou, my Saviour Christ, art gone before!
In mind and heart
Let me dwell always, only, where Thou art.

Oh, let me give
Out of the gifts Thou freely givest;
Oh, let me live
With life abundantly because Thou livest;
Oh, make me shine
In darkest places, for Thy light is mine;
Oh, let me be
A faithful witness for Thy truth and Thee.

Oh, let me show
The strong reality of gospel story;
Oh, let me go
From strength to strength, from glory unto glory;
Oh, let me sing
For very joy, because Thou art my King;
Oh, let me praise
Thy love and faithfulness through all my days.

—FRANCES RIDLEY HAVERGAL

## AN EASTER PRAYER

God's blessing rest upon you
This happy Easter Day,
*And go quickly, and tell his disciples that he is risen from the dead.*
—Matt. 28:7

God make His joy to shine
  As sunlight on your way;
God fill your heart with song
  So glad it will not cease;
God bless you every day
  With love and joy and peace.

—AUTHOR UNKNOWN

## MY RISEN LORD

My risen Lord, I feel thy strong protection;
I see thee stand among the graves today;
I am the Way, the Life, the Resurrection,
    I hear thee say,
And all the burdens I have carried sadly
Grow light as blossoms on an April day;
My cross becomes a staff, I journey gladly
    This Easter day.

—AUTHOR UNKNOWN

## MY EASTER PRAYER

May you walk a little surer
  On the path that lies before,
May you see a little clearer
  May you trust a little more.
May you come a little closer
  To the Lord of Love Divine,
That your heart may sing for gladness,
  Is this Easter prayer of mine.

—AUTHOR UNKNOWN

*Now is Christ risen from the dead, and become the first-fruits of them
that slept.* —I Cor. 25:20

# THANKSGIVING

*Enter into his gates with thanksgiving, and into his courts with praise: be thankful unto him, and bless his name.*

—Ps. 100:4

## GRATITUDE

I thank You for these gifts, dear God,
    Upon Thanksgiving Day—
For love and laughter and the faith
    That makes me kneel to pray.

For life that lends me happiness,
    And sleep that gives me rest,
These are the gifts that keep my heart
    Serene within my breast.

Love, laughter, faith and life and sleep,
    We own them, every one—
They carry us along the road
    That leads from sun to sun.

—MARGARET E. SANGSTER

## LET US COME BEFORE HIS PRESENCE

Psalm 95:2

Let us come before His presence
    With thanksgiving—on this day
When all things attest His bounty
    By so lavish a display;

*Let us come before his presence with thanksgiving, and make a joyful noise unto him with psalms.*    —Ps. 95:2

Where our loved ones gather with us
  At the feast He has prepared
From the harvest of His planting—
  That with all it may be shared.

Let us come before His presence—
  Who again has brought us through
To this day so crowned with blessings.
  It was little we could do
To dispel the clouds about us,
  Vain we struggled through the night
Of depression, till we sought Him
  And He led us to the Light.

Let us come before His presence—
  Giving thanks for all we own;
Life, love, liberty, and friendship;
  All the riches He has sown
In the earth for us to harvest.
  But the day is not complete
As a day of true thanksgiving—
  Till we lay all at His feet.

Let us come before His presence
  With thanksgiving—on this day
When all things attest His bounty
  By so lavish a display.
Let us place upon His altar
  All we have, that we may share
With our less provided brothers
  Of our plenty—this our prayer.
                              —WILLIAM LUDLUM

*O give thanks unto the Lord, for he is good; for his mercy endureth
for ever.*                                    —Ps. 107:1

## A HYMN OF THANKSGIVING

For all the blessings of the year,
   For sunshine and for showers,
For seedtime and for harvest rich,
   For bird songs and for flowers
From hearts overflowing with Thy praise
Accept, O Lord, the thanks we raise.

And for the gift of Thy dear Son,
   From sin to set us free,
No tongue can tell, no words express
   The praise we offer Thee,
For Christ, who came for us to die,
Accept our thanks, O God on high.

For grace and glory which He gives,
   For pardon, joy, and peace,
Our voices raise to Thee, O God,
   In songs that never cease,
For victory amid the strife
Accept our thanks, O Lord of Life.

And for the hope of His return,
   Dear Lord, Thy Name we praise,
With longing hearts we watch and wait
   For that great Day of Days,
For Christ, our coming Lord and King
To Thee, O God, our thanks we bring.

                —ALICE E. SHERWOOD

## OUR REFUGE AND STRENGTH

Lord God of hosts, we render thanks
   For all Thy mercies sure;

*O give thanks unto the Lord; call upon his name; make known his
deeds among the people.*            —Ps. 105:1

Thy tender love environs us
   And will through life endure.

Teach us to know Thy perfect will,
   Humble and meek to be;
May we, in gladness, praise Thy Name
   Throughout eternity.

Lord God of hosts, we offer thanks
   And call upon Thy Name;
A psalm of praise to Thee we sing,
   Thy wondrous love proclaim.

Thou art our refuge and our strength,
   There is no other power;
If sudden danger threatens us
   We find in Thee a tower.

Lord God of hosts, we proffer praise,
   Direct us on our way;
With grateful hearts we worship Thee
   On this Thanksgiving Day.
—GRENVILLE KLEISER

## WE THANK THEE

Father, we thank Thee:
For peace within our favored land,
For plenty from Thy bounteous hand,
For means to give to those in need,
For grace to help in thought and deed,
For faith to walk, our hands in Thine,
For truth to know Thy law divine,
For strength to work with voice and pen,

*I will offer to thee the sacrifice of thanksgiving.*   —Ps. 116:17

For love to serve our fellow men,
For light the goal ahead to see,
For life to use alone for Thee,
Father, we thank Thee.

—GRENVILLE KLEISER

## PRAYER AT THANKSGIVING TIME

Thank God for home,
And crisp, fair weather,
And loving hearts
That meet together—
And red, ripe fruit
And golden grain—
And dear Thanksgiving
Come again!

—NANCY BYRD TURNER

## THANKSGIVING DAY GRACE

Our Father, fill our hearts, we pray,
With gratitude Thanksgiving Day;
For food and raiment Thou dost give,
That we in comfort here may live.

With bread of life our spirits feed
And grant to us the grace we need,
Guide Thou our feet lest they should stray
From paths of righteousness away.

True service may we render Thee
In love and deep humility;
Deliver us from every sin,
In His dear name we ask. *Amen.*

—LUTHER B. CROSS

*The Lord hath done great things for us; whereof we are glad.*

—Ps. 126:3

## THANKSGIVING DAY

I thank Thee for so many things—
Through autumn, winter, all the springs
And summers, every day holds cause
For thankfulness. Then grant me pause
At each new silvering dawn to say:
This, Lord, is my Thanksgiving Day.

—MARIE BARTON

# CHRISTMAS

*Glory to God in the highest, and on earth peace, good will to-*
*ward men.*

—Luke 2:14

## FOR CHRISTMAS EVE—A PRAYER

O Lord, there sit apart in lonely places,
    At this, the gladdest time of all the year,
Some stricken ones with sad and weary faces,
    To whom the thought of Christmas brings no cheer.
For these, O Father, our petition hear
And send the pitying Christ Child near.

And there are tempted souls this night, still waging
    Such desperate warfare with all evil powers.
Anthems of peace, while the dread strife is raging,
    Sound but a mockery through their midnight hours.
For these, O Father, our petition hear,
And send Thy tempted, sinless Christ Child very near.

Lord, some sit by lonely hearthstones sobbing,
    Who feel this night all earthly love denied,

*And thou shalt call his name Jesus: for he shall save his people from*
*their sins.*                                          —Matt. 1:21

41

Who hear but dirges in the loud bell's throbbing
  For loved ones lost who blessed last Christmastide.
For these, O Father, our petition hear
And send the loving Christ Child very near.

—AUTHOR UNKNOWN

## PRAYER ON CHRISTMAS EVE

O wondrous night of star and song,
  O blessed Christmas night!
Lord, make me feel my whole life long
  Its loveliness and light!
So all the years my heart shall thrill
Remembering angels on a hill,
And one lone star shall bless me still
  On every Christmas night!

—NANCY BYRD TURNER

## PEACE ON EARTH

O Thou good Giver of all gifts,
  At this hushed Christmastide,
Look on a troubled world that lifts
  Her cup unsatisfied,
And brim her joylessness again
With "peace on earth, good will to men!"

Oh, shrive all hearts of greed and wrong
  And whiten them with love;
Give to the sons of men a song
  Like unto that above,
A Christmas song dispelling sadness,
Recharging Earth with Heaven's gladness—

*Fear not: for, behold, I bring you good tidings of great joy, which shall
be to all people.*                                    —Luke 2:10

A paean to sweep out warring hate
   From every land and race,
And heal before it be too late
   A wrangling world's scarred face—
O Thou great Giver of all good,
Grant peace this day, and brotherhood!
               —Marie Barton

## THE PERFECT GIFT

We worship Thee, O Son of God,
   On this most holy day,
Who came to earth a little Babe
   And in a manger lay;
Thou who didst leave Thy Heavenly home
   To break earth's chains of night,
Whose advent brought a world new hope,
   Changed darkness into light.

The angel of the Lord appeared
   As shepherds vigil kept,
Proclaimed good tidings of great joy
   To man, which 'round them slept.
The heavenly host sang praise to God
   And peace, good will on earth;
The shepherds sought the Christ Child's bed
   And marveled at His birth.

As wise men traveled from the East,
   Led by that gleaming star,
And brought their precious gifts to Thee
   From their own lands afar;

*For unto you is born this day, in the city of David, a Saviour, which is*
*Christ the Lord.*                   —Luke 2:11

So we to Thee would homage bring
  And sing that heavenly strain
Of peace on earth, good will to men,
  The world so needs again.

At this glad time we too would bring
  Our greatest gift to Thee;
Lord, first ourselves, then all we have,
  Our perfect gift would be.
Wilt Thou through us shine forth to men
  Who need Thy light so clear;
Use us, our money, talents, time,
  In Thy sweet service here.

                    —JULIA BENSON PARKER

## A CHRISTMAS PRAYER

Lord, let my heart be always young at Christmas.
  Lord, never let my eyes grow old or be
Dim to the grandeur of the winter season
  That brings with it the glittering Christmas tree.
Let me always feel the poetry of the snowfall
  And of myriad lights from firesides gleaming through
The windows where the faces of expectant children
  Are lovely as June roses wet with dew.

Let me feel the childish thrill of Christmas
  That lives in knowing "Santa Claus will know,"
And never let my ears grow dull to hearing
  The melody of sweet carols 'cross the snow.
Lord, never let me grow too wise or modern
  To love the Story which the years have not undone;

*And they came with haste, and found Mary, and Joseph, and the babe
lying in a manger.*                    —Luke 2:16

44

I just want to be a child with Mary's Child
　And in simple faith to trust the Father's Son.
　　　　　　　　　　　—RUBY DELL BAUGHER


## A CHRISTMAS SONG

God, give me a song for the world that's glad
　When cometh the Christmastide,
For fain would I teach the world a song
　Joyous and free and clear and strong,
Gladness to bring to the Christmas throng,
　To add to the joys of joyous men,
　Full in Excelsis sing again.
　　Low and sweet, low and sweet
Down in my heart these words repeat:
　　Jesus the Saviour is born!

God, give me a song for the world that's sad
　When cometh the Christmastide,
For fain would I teach the world a song
　Cheering and sweet, in comfort strong,
To ease life's hurt and to right life's wrong;
　For many there be that walk this day
　With hearts attired in a lonesome gray;
　　Low and sweet, low and sweet,
Down in my heart these words repeat:
　　Jesus the Saviour is born!

God, give me a song for the hearts of men
　When cometh the Christmastide,
For fain would I stop earth's hurrying feet,
　Jostle and rush with noise replete,
And once again those words repeat

*And the shepherds returned, glorifying and praising God for all the*
*things that they had heard and seen.*　　　　　—Luke 2:20

To sad and to glad as they trudge along
And bid them echo the Yuletide song;
Low and sweet, low and sweet,
Sad and glad in their hearts repeat:
Jesus the Saviour is born!

—RUTH WINANT WHEELER

## A PRAYER AT CHRISTMAS TIME

Lord, in all the stir
When Christmas comes around,
The games and the greetings,
The songs and the meetings,
The toys and joys and shining trees,
The carols' sweet sound—

Father, in the midst of these,
Let us not forget
The fair Star of Christmas,
The Star that cannot set.
Let us lift our hearts and say,
"Glory be to God in heaven,
On Christmas Day!"

—NANCY BYRD TURNER

## CHRISTMAS

Saviour, on Thy birthday dear
    Make us to remember
How the star's clear light was shed
Down upon Thy manger bed,
With the angels bending low,
Far away and long ago,
    One December.

*When they saw the star, they rejoiced.*                —Matt. 2:10

Saviour, when Thy birthday falls,
   Make us to remember
Other children near and far
Who should see the Christmas star,
Hear the song and love the light
Of Thy birthday fair and bright
   In December!

        —NANCY BYRD TURNER

# The Small Circle

HOME

BRIDE AND GROOM

FATHER

MOTHER

CHILDREN

FRIENDS

# The Small Circle

## HOME

*Let them learn first to show piety at home, . . . . for that is good and acceptable before God.*

*—I Tim. 5:4*

### GOD BLESS OUR HOME

Eternal Father, who hast given
To homes on earth foretaste of heaven,
Whose gentle Spirit from above
Doth breathe Thy peace in hearts that love;
  While here we bide, or far we roam,
  Hear this our prayer: God Bless Our Home!

O Saviour, who didst smile to see
The bridal feast in Galilee,
Whose grace we crave on all who bow,
For life and death to take their vow;
  While here we bide, or far we roam,
  Hear this our prayer: God Bless Our Home!

O Tender Shepherd, who dost hold
Each little lamb within Thy fold,
With rod and staff who followest still
The wandering sheep o'er vale and hill;
  While here we bide, or far we roam,
  Hear this our prayer: God Bless Our Home!

*Then saith he to the disciple, Behold thy mother! And from that hour that disciple took her unto his own home.*     —John 19:27

Eternal Father, ever near,
With arm outstretched and listening ear,
Whose mercy keeps, whose power defends
Our sons, our daughters, and our friends,
  While here we bide, or far we roam,
  Hear this our prayer: God Bless Our Home.
                              —ROBERT FREEMAN


## LINES FOR A FRIEND'S HOUSE

God bless this house and all within it,
Let no harsh spirit enter in it,
Let none approach who would betray,
None with a bitter word to say.
Shield it from harm and sorrow's sting,
Here let the children's laughter ring,
Grant that these friends from year to year
Shall build their happiest memories here.

God bless this house and those who love it,
Fair be the skies which bend above it.
May never anger's thoughtless word
Within these sheltering walls be heard,
May all who rest beside this fire
And then depart, glad thoughts inspire,
And make them feel who close the door,
Friendship has graced their home once more.

God bless this house and those who keep it,
In the sweet oils of gladness steep it,
Endow these walls with lasting wealth,
The light of love, the glow of health,

*The Lord is good to all; and his tender mercies are over all his works.*
                              —Ps. 145:9

The palm of peace, the charm of mirth,
Good friends to sit around the hearth,
And with each nightfall perfect rest—
Here let them live their happiest.

—EDGAR A. GUEST


## DEDICATION

O thou whose gracious presence blest
  The home at Bethany,
This shelter from the world's unrest,
This home made ready for its Guest,
  We dedicate to thee.

We build an altar here, and pray
  That thou wilt show thy face.
Dear Lord, if thou wilt come to stay,
This home we consecrate today
  Will be a holy place.

—LOUIS F. BENSON


## PRAYER FOR A LITTLE HOME

God send us a little home
To come back to when we roam—
Low walls and fluted tiles;
Wide windows, a view for miles;
Red firelight and deep chairs;
Small white beds upstairs;
Great talk in little nooks;
Dim colors, rows of books;
One picture on each wall;
Not many things at all.

*He entered into a certain village: and a certain woman, named Martha, received him into her house.* —Luke 10:38

God send us a little ground—
Tall trees standing round,
Homely flowers in brown sod,
Overhead Thy stars, O God!
God bless, when winds blow,
Our home and all we know.

—FLORENCE BONE

## HOUSE BLESSING

Bless the four corners of this house,
   And be the lintel blest;
And bless the hearth, and bless the board,
   And bless each place of rest;

And bless the door that opens wide
   To stranger, as to kin;
And bless each crystal windowpane
   That lets the starlight in;

And bless the rooftree overhead,
   And every sturdy wall.
The peace of man, the peace of God,
   The peace of love on all.

—ARTHUR GUITERMAN

## HYMN FOR A HOUSEHOLD

Lord Christ, beneath thy starry dome
We light this flickering lamp of home,
And where bewildering shadows throng
Uplift our prayer and evensong.

*And Jesus said unto him, This day is salvation come to this house.*
—Luke 19:9

Dost thou, with heaven in thy ken
Seek still a dwelling-place with men,
Wandering the world in ceaseless quest?
O Man of Nazareth, be our guest!

Lord Christ, the bird his nest has found,
The fox is sheltered in his ground,
But dost thou still this dark earth tread
And have no place to lay thy head?
Shepherd of mortals, here behold
A little flock, a wayside fold
That wait thy presence to be blest—
O Man of Nazareth, be our guest!
—DANIEL HENDERSON

## DEDICATION OF A HOME

Enter with us, Lord, we pray,
This our new-built house today,
Bless with Thine own love each room
Unto all of us to whom
This is home, a refuge sweet
From life's burden and its heat.

"Not our own," Lord, help us make
This our house's motto; take
All the mean self-centeredness
From our souls, and help us bless
All who enter at our doors.
Make the feet that touch our floors
Tread more gladly.   Help us share
Light and food and easy chair,

*Zacchaeus, make haste, and come down, for to day I must abide at
thy house.* —Luke 19:5

All home comforts, in Thy name.
Make them glad because they came.

Let no weary, troubled guest
Fail of finding peace and rest
At our table. Though it be
Simple, let it speak of Thee.
Sharing, may we all be fed
By Thyself, O Living Bread.
— BERTHA GERNEAUX WOODS

## O HAPPY HOME

O happy home, where Thou art loved the dearest,
  Thou loving Friend, and Saviour of our race,
And where among the guests there never cometh
  One who can hold such high and honored place!

O happy home, where two in heart united
  In holy faith and blessed hope are one,
Whom death a little while alone divideth,
  And cannot end the union here begun!

O happy home, where Thou art not forgotten
  When joy is overflowing, full, and free;
O happy home, where every wounded spirit
  Is brought, Physician, Comforter, to Thee—

Until at last, when earth's day's work is ended
  All meet Thee in the blessed home above,
From whence Thou camest, where Thou hast ascended,
  Thy everlasting home of peace and love!
— CARL J. P. SPITTA

*In my Father's house are many mansions: if it were not so, I would
have told you. I go to prepare a place for you.* —John 14:2

# BRIDE AND GROOM

*Therefore shall a man leave his father and his mother, and shall cleave unto his wife.*

—Gen. 2:24

## PRAYER AT A WEDDING

Thou God, whose high, eternal Love
    Is the only blue sky of our life,
Clear all the Heaven that bends above
    The life-road of this man and wife.

May these two lives be but one note
    In the world's strange-sounding harmony,
Whose sacred music e'er shall float
    Through every discord up to Thee.

As when from separate stars two beams
    Unite to form one tender ray:
As when two sweet but shadowy dreams
    Explain each other in the day:

So may these two dear hearts one light
    Emit, and each interpret each.
Let an angel come and dwell to-night
    In this dear double-heart, and teach!

—SIDNEY LANIER

## A MARRIAGE PRAYER

Lord of Life, look smiling down
Upon this pair; with choicest blessings crown

*Husbands, love your wives, even as Christ also loved the church, and gave himself for it.* —Eph. 5:25

57

Their love; the beauty of the Flower bring
Back to the bud again in some new spring!
Long may they walk the blessed life together
With wedded hearts that still make golden weather
And keep the chill of winter far aloof
With inward warmth when snow is on the roof;
Wed in that sweet forever of Love's kiss,
Like two rich notes made one in bridal bliss.
We would not pray that sorrow ne'er may shed
Her dews along the pathway they must tread;
The sweetest flowers would never bloom at all
If no least rain of tears did ever fall.
In joy the soul is bearing human fruit;
In grief it may be taking divine root.
Come joy or grief, nestle them near to Thee
In happy love twine for eternity!

—GERALD MASSEY

## PRAYER FOR A BRIDE

She is so beautiful, so pure, dear God.
    He is so tall, so fearless as they stand
Together at the threshold of their dreams.
    Oh, grant them length of days within the land.

Oh, always may her shining eyes be proud
    Of him to whom she plights her troth today.
And may he be as tender through the years—
    Theirs be a love time cannot take away!

Teach them, our Father, marriage is much more
    Than one low-roofed, small house where two shall live.
More than new rooms resplendent with bright gifts
    Which happy friends, well-wishing them, may give.

*Beloved, if God so loved us, we ought also to love one another.*
—I John 4:11

58

Love bears all things, believeth, hopes, endures
  With stronger bonds than vows or nuptial kiss,
Love vaunteth not itself, seeks not its own,
  Love never faileth. . . . . Father, teach them this!
              —HELEN WELSHIMER

## PRAYER FOR HELP

God bless our home, and help us
  To love each other true;
To make our home the kind of place
  Where everything we do
Is filled with love and kindness,
  A dwelling place for Thee,
And help us, God, each moment,
  To live most helpfully.
              —AUTHOR UNKNOWN

## PRAYER FOR ANY BRIDE AND GROOM

May passing years send happiness
  Upon you two together,
And kindly Fortune smile on you
  In every kind of weather.

Should dark'ning hours threaten you,
  Or frowning skies bring rain,
Be sure that in a little while
  The sun will shine again.

The sun ne'er shines so radiantly
  As when, at evening hour,
It sets behind storm-scattered clouds
  That erstwhile held the shower.

*Beloved, let us love one another: for love is of God.*   —I John 4:7

So may the storms that press your way
 Be driven far and wide,
Yet leave some clouds to glorify
 The sun at eventide.

—J. Shenton Lodge


## PRAYER FOR A BRIDE'S HOUSE

She is so young, dear Lord, so very young;
 She is so wide-eyed and naïvely sweet;
She does not dream of great rooms, draped and hung
 With master paintings, rugs where some queen's feet
Have lightly trod.  She dreams of this instead:
 A small, new house with freshly painted floors,
With hand-stitched curtains, and above her head
 Bright dishes gleaming through wee cupboard doors.
She'll learn, some day, the value of old things,
 When eagerness is still, and she is wise—
Knowing the disillusionment time brings—
 But now, there's so much springtime in her eyes,
And this is her first house—Whate'er You do,
Let everything about it, Lord, be new!

—Christie Lund


## PRAYER AT A WEDDING

Giver of good and perfect gifts,
Father and Shepherd of our souls,
Source of all life and joy;
Of Thee the family in heaven and earth is named;
From Thee come love and trust,
And all that knits together kindred minds
In unity of purpose and of thought.

*My little children, let us not love in word, neither in tongue; but in deed and in truth.* —I John 3:18

Thou settest us in homes—in little groups—
In which we learn to share our joys and griefs—
"Two heads in counsel, two beside the hearth,
Two in the liberal offices of life."

Bless Thou the tie that now unites these hearts;
May their affection never change save as it grows
The deeper with the years.
Together they are young; so, too, may they grow old,
In step, each with the other, comrades all the way,
Through life's long march unto the journey's end.
If paths are rough and winds blow cold,
May they the closer draw, and hand in hand,
Appear before Thy face, serene and unashamed.
Grant Thou Thy help to keep inviolate their vows;
Endow them with the noble power to give and take—
The grace of "yieldingness"—the will to seek
Each in the other's self, self's perfect complement:
So may they come to know the meaning of the word
He spoke who said, "They two shall be as one."

—CHARLES CARROLL ALBERTSON

## FATHER

*I have written unto you, fathers, because ye have known him
that is from the beginning.*

—I John 2:14

### A FATHER'S PRAYER

Father, today I bring to Thee
This boy of mine whom Thou hast made;

*When he was yet a great way off, his father saw him, and had com-
passion, and ran, and fell on his neck, and kissed him.*

—Luke 15:20

In everything he looks to me;
    In turn I look to Thee for aid.

He knows not all that is before;
    He little dreams of hidden snares;
He holds my hand, and o'er and o'er
    I find myself beset with fears.

Father, as this boy looks up to me
    For guidance, and my help implores,
I bring him now in prayer to Thee;
    He trusts my strength and I trust Yours.

Hold Thou my hand as I hold his,
    And so guide that I may guide;
Teach me, Lord, that I may teach,
    And keep me free from foolish pride.

Help me to help this boy of mine,
    To be to him a father true;
Hold me, Lord, for every thing,
    As fast I hold my boy for You.
             —Mouzon W. Brabham

## A FATHER'S PRAYER

When all is still within these walls,
And Thy sweet sleep through darkness falls
On little hearts that trust in me,
However bitter toil may be,
For length of days, O Lord! on Thee
        My spirit calls.

*And, ye fathers, provoke not your children to wrath: but bring them up in the nurture and admonition of the Lord.*    —Eph. 6:4

Their daily need by day enthralls
My hand and brain, but when night falls
And leaves the questioning spirit free
To brood upon the days to be,
For time and strength, O Lord! on Thee
My spirit calls.
—Author Unknown

## FATHER-PRAYER

Lord God, who let Your baby Son
Pass earthward, where His joys were few,
To a hard death when all was done,
And very far away from You—

Lord God, whose Son went steadily
Down the hard road He had to tread,
Guard my son too, that he may be
Strong in his hours of doubt and dread.
—Margaret Widdemer

## MOTHER

*Her children arise up, and call her blessed.*

—Prov. 31:28

### A PRAYER FOR MOTHERS

God give us Mothers, this we plead,
To still our woes in hours of need.
To hush with gentle accents blest,
The bitter cry.  And soothe to rest

*Honour thy father and thy mother; that thy days may be long upon
the land which the Lord thy God giveth thee.*      —Exod. 20:12

63

The weary soul.  For this we pray,
To Mother's God on Mother's Day.
—John F. Todd


## A MOTHER SPEAKS

Father in Heaven, make me wise,
  So that my gaze may never meet
A question in my children's eyes.
  God keep me always kind and sweet,

And patient, too, before their need;
  Let each vexation know its place,
Let gentleness be all my creed,
  Let laughter live upon my face!

A mother's day is very long,
  There are so many things to do!
But never let me lose my song
  Before the hardest day is through.
—Margaret E. Sangster


## MOTHER-PRAYER

Lord, make my loving a guard for them
  Day and night,
Let never pathway be hard for them;
  Keep all bright;
Let not harsh touch of a thorn for them
  Wound their ease—
All of the pain I have borne for them
  Spare to these!

*As one whom his mother comforteth, so will I comfort you.*
—Isa. 66:13

64

So I would pray for them,
Kneeling to God
Night and day for them.

Lord, let the pain life must bring to them
      Make them strong,
Keep their hearts white though grief cling to them
      All life long,
Let all the joys Thou dost keep from them
      At Thy will
Give to them power to reap from them
      Courage still.

So I must ask for them,
Leaving to God
His own task for them.

            —MARGARET WIDDEMER

## THE MOTHER'S TRUST
### Exodus 12:3, 11, 13

Beneath the bloodstained lintel I with my children stand;
A messenger of evil is passing through the land.
There is no other refuge from the destroyer's face;
Beneath the bloodstained lintel shall be our hiding-place.

The Lamb of God has suffered, our sins and griefs He bore;
By faith the blood is sprinkled above our dwelling's door.
The foe who seeks to enter doth fear that sacred sign;
Tonight the bloodstained lintel shall shelter me and mine.

My Saviour, for my dear ones I claim Thy promise true;
The Lamb is "for the household"—the children's Saviour too.

*Blessed is the man that trusteth in the Lord, and whose hope the
Lord is.*         —Jer. 17:7

65

On earth the little children once felt Thy touch divine;
Beneath the bloodstained lintel Thy blessing give to mine.

O Thou who gave them, guard them—those wayward little feet,
The wilderness before them, the ills of life to meet.
My mother-love is helpless, I trust them to Thy care!
Beneath the bloodstained lintel, oh, keep me ever there!

The faith I rest upon Thee Thou wilt not disappoint;
With wisdom, Lord, to train them my shrinking heart anoint.
Without my children, Father, I cannot see Thy face;
I plead the bloodstained lintel, Thy covenant of grace.

O wonderful Redeemer, who suffered for our sake,
When o'er the guilty nations the judgment storm shall break,
With joy from that safe shelter may we then meet Thine eye,
Beneath the bloodstained lintel, my children, Lord, and I.
—AUTHOR UNKNOWN

## PRAYER FOR A COLLEGE GIRL

So dear, so dear she is to me,
    This child who leaves my side today!
But dearer still, O Lord, to Thee,
    And so with confidence I pray.

She'll weary as the weeks go by,
    And gay adjustment lose its zest;
But sure of Thine approving eye
    May she have quiet rest.

If disappointment's sword should fall,
    Or sorrow flash from a clear sky,

*O Lord, my strength, and my fortress, and my refuge in the day of
affliction.* —Jer. 16:19

66

May she have grace to suffer all,
    Sure of Thy sympathy.

She will have hours of lonely doubt;
    Let her be calm through all suspense,
And work her own salvation out,
    Sure of Thy providence.

If to the battle she must thrill,
    Then may she fight right faithfully,
Or tempted in the desert, still
    Be sure of victory.
                —ELLA BROADUS ROBERTSON

# CHILDREN

*Suffer the little children to come unto me, and forbid them not; for of such is the kingdom of God.*
                —Mark 10:14

Lord, who lovest little children,
Hear us as we pray to Thee.
                —M. R.

## MORNING PRAYERS

Now I wake and see the light,
'Tis God that kept me through the night.
To Him I lift my voice and pray
That He will keep me through the day.
                —AUTHOR UNKNOWN

I thank Thee, Father, for my rest;
Help me today to do my best.

*My voice shalt thou hear in the morning, O Lord.*    —Ps. 5:3

Glad and happy would I be,
So I pray for help from Thee.
—Author Unknown

Heavenly Father, hear our prayer;
Keep us in Thy loving care.
Guard us through the livelong day,
In our work and in our play.
Keep us pure and strong and true,
In everything we say and do.
—Author Unknown

## EVENING PRAYER

Now I lay me down to sleep,
I pray Thee, Lord, Thy child to keep.
Thy love go with me all the night
And wake me with the morning light.
—Author Unknown

## A CHILD'S PRAYER

Dear Lord we thank Thee for this day,
For food, for fun, for work, for play.
—William L. Stidger

## AN EVENING PRAYER

Jesus, tender Shepherd, hear me;
  Bless Thy little lamb to-night;
Through the darkness be Thou near me;
  Keep me safe till morning light.

All this day Thy hand has led me,
  And I thank Thee for Thy care;

*Abide with us: for it is toward evening.*          —Luke 24:29

Thou hast clothed me, warmed and fed me;
  Listen to my evening prayer.


Let my sins be all forgiven;
  Bless the friends I love so well;
Take me, when I die, to heaven,
  Happy there with Thee to dwell.

—MARY LUNDIE DUNCAN


## I'M GLAD

I've tried, dear God,
To do my best;
I've had
A happy day;
There's something sings
Inside of me,
And makes me want
To pray.

—ELIZABETH McE. SHIELDS


## BLESSINGS AT TABLE

Once more, the head, O Lord, we bow,
And for our bread we thank Thee now.

—AUTHOR UNKNOWN


Thou art great, and Thou art good,
And we thank Thee for this food.
By Thy hand must all be fed;
Give us, Lord, our daily bread.

—AUTHOR UNKNOWN

*Sing unto the Lord with thanksgiving.*          —Ps. 147:7

## FOR ALL OUR LOVED ONES

For all our loved ones do we pray,
For those at home who every day
    Surround us with their care;

For friends so true and neighbors good,
For all who work to give us food,
    Our thanks to God we bear.

With those who lack what we enjoy,
With every needy girl and boy
    Help us, Lord, to share.

For children far beyond the sea,
For all who do not know of Thee,
    Hear, Lord, our humble prayer.

—AUTHOR UNKNOWN

## OUR FATHER, AS WE START THE DAY

Our Father, as we start the day,
We think of children far away
In other lands across the sea.
Help us their loving friends to be.
Help all Thy children everywhere
To share Thee and Thy loving care.

—AGNES SMYTH KELSEY

## A PRAYER FOR MY PLAYMATES

Lord, bless my playmates,
    This I pray.
Bless us together
    When we play;

*The Lord bless thee, and keep thee.*             —Num. 6:24

Bless us apart;
And make us know
Thy love, wherever
We may go.
—AUTHOR UNKNOWN

## IN ILLNESS

Lord Jesus, You were always good
To everyone in pain,
Please think of me while I am ill
And make me well again.
—AUTHOR UNKNOWN

## GOD IS NEAR

Sometimes when morning lights the sky
And gladness fills the air,
I feel like telling things to God,
He seems so very near.

Sometimes when flowers are in bloom
And birds are singing clear,
I feel like singing things to God,
He must be very near.

Sometimes when trees are standing tall
With branches in the air,
I feel like saying things to God,
I know He must be near.

Sometimes when work and play are done
And evening stars appear,
I feel like whisp'ring things to God,
He is so very near.
—ELIZABETH McE. SHIELDS

*Call unto me, and I will answer thee.*　　　　　—Jer. 33:3

## I STRETCH MY THOUGHTS

O God, I have to stretch my thoughts to think of You,
For You are great, as great as all the world,
And I cannot imagine all the world.
I can only understand the part I see
And think, "like that, and more of that, and more, and more,"
Until it seems to go right on forever.
I stand on tiptoe and reach up and up,
Trying to see beyond the clouds and sky,
And think, "The world is taller still than that,
And God is greater even than the world!"

—JEANETTE E. PERKINS

## SOCIAL HYMN FOR CHILDREN

We thank Thee, God, for eyes to see
  The beauty of the earth;
For ears to hear the words of love
  And happy sounds of mirth;
For minds that find new thoughts to think,
  New wonders to explore;
For health and freedom to enjoy
  The good Thou hast in store.

—JEANETTE E. PERKINS

## FATHER, WE THANK THEE

Father, we thank Thee for the night,
And for the pleasant morning light;
For rest and food and loving care,
And all that makes the day so fair.

*Bless the Lord, O my soul, and forget not all his benefits.*

—Ps. 103:2

72

Help us to do the things we should,
To be to others kind and good;
In all we do in work or play,
To grow more loving every day.
— REBECCA J. WESTON

## THE EXTRA PRAYER

Sometimes I say an extra prayer,
    Besides the one for which I kneel.
I stand and look up at the stars,
    And tell our Father how I feel.

I do not ask for anything;
    I just feel happy through and through.
I let my heart give thanks and sing,
    Till all the world seems good and true.
— ANNIE WILLIS McCULLOUGH

## OUR THANKS

For home and friends and loved ones dear
    We thank Thee, heavenly Father;
For power to walk and see and hear,
    We thank Thee, heavenly Father;
For food and drink and clothes to wear
For all Thy loving help and care,
And for Thy goodness everywhere,
    We thank Thee, heavenly Father.
— NAN F. WEEKS

## NOW IN THE DAYS OF YOUTH

Now in the days of youth,
    When life flows fresh and free,

*O give thanks unto the Lord, for he is good.*          — Ps. 107:1

73

Thou Lord of all our hearts and lives
　　We give ourselves to thee;
Our fervent gift receive,
　　And fit us to fulfill,
Through all our days, in all our ways,
　　Our Heavenly Father's will.

Teach us where'er we live,
　　To act as in thy sight,
And do what thou wouldst have us do
　　With radiant delight;
Not choosing what is great,
　　Nor spurning what is small,
But take as from thy hands our tasks
　　And glorify them all.

Teach us to love the true,
　　The beautiful and pure,
And let us not for one short hour
　　An evil thought endure.
But give us grace to stand
　　Decided, brave and strong,
The lovers of all holy things,
　　The foes of all things wrong.
　　　　　　　　　—WALTER J. MATHAMS


## YOUTH'S PRAYER

To build a life that's clean, upright, secure,
God's Temple that will through the years endure;
To walk courageously, steadfast and sure;
　　　This is my prayer.

*Remember now thy Creator in the days of thy youth.*—Eccles. 12:1

To teach a war-torn world the fruits of peace;
To plead that cruelty and hate must cease,
That earth might see goodwill and love increase;
      This is my prayer.

To dedicate my life, my youth, my all
To Christ, and then in answer to His call,
Be faithful to each task—the large, the small;
      This is my prayer.

        —GEORGE W. WISEMAN

# FRIENDS

*If we walk in the light, as he is in the light, we have fellowship one with another.*

        —I John 1:7

## IN GRATITUDE FOR FRIENDS

I thank you, God in Heaven, for friends.
When morning wakes, when daytime ends,
   I have the consciousness
Of loving hands that touch my own,
Of tender glance and gentle tone,
   Of thoughts that cheer and bless!

If sorrow comes to me I know
That friends will walk the way I go,
   And, as the shadows fall,
I know that I will raise my eyes
And see—ah, hope that never dies!—
   The dearest Friend of All.

        —MARGARET E. SANGSTER

*And the Lord turned the captivity of Job, when he prayed for his friends.*     —Job 42:10

## PRAYER FOR A FRIEND

Friend of the Changeless Love,
  Be with my friend today;
I may not serve her need,
  For I am far away;
But Thou canst be with her,
  Forever at her side,
To give her strength and peace;
  To comfort, guard, and guide.
Her Friend and mine, to Thee I pray,
Oh, be Thou with my friend today!

God of the Changeless Years,
  Be with my friend for aye,
Through years that give with lavish hand
  And years that take away;
For Thou art still the same
  Though all around be strange,
Thy love and care remain
  Though all beside may change;
All else may fail or pass away—
Oh, be Thou with my friend for aye!

—ANNIE JOHNSON FLINT

## THE PRAYER PERFECT

Dear Lord! kind Lord!
  Gracious Lord! I pray
Thou wilt look on all I love,
  Tenderly today!
Weed their hearts of weariness;
  Scatter every care
Down a wake of angel-wings
  Winnowing the air.

*Brethren, pray for us.*                    —I Thess. 5: 25

Bring unto the sorrowing
  All release from pain;
Let the lips of laughter
  Overflow again;
And with all the needy
  O divide, I pray,
This vast treasure of content
  That is mine to-day!
                —JAMES WHITCOMB RILEY


## A FRIEND'S PRAYER

The Lord preserve thy going out,
  The Lord preserve thy coming in;
God send His angels round about,
  To keep thy soul from every sin.
                —AUTHOR UNKNOWN


## IN EXTREMITY

Think on him, Lord! we ask thy aid
  In life's most dreaded extremity:
For evil days have come to him,
  Who in his youth remembered thee.

Look on him, Lord! for heart and flesh,
  Alike, must fail without thy grace:
Part back the clouds, that he may see
  The brightness of his Father's face.

Speak to him, Lord! as thou didst talk
  To Adam, in the Garden's shade,
And grant it unto him to hear
  Thy voice, and not to be afraid.

*The Lord make his face shine upon thee, and be gracious unto thee.*
                —Num. 6:25

77

Support him, Lord! that he may come,
　Leaning on thee, in faith sublime,
Up to that awful landmark, set
　Between eternity and time.

And, Lord, if it must be that we
　Shall walk with him no more below,
Reach out of heaven thy loving hand,
　And lead him where we cannot go.
　　　　　　　　　　—PHOEBE CARY

# The Large Circle

THE CHURCH

THE MINISTER

THE TEACHER

MISSIONS

THOSE WHO FLY

THOSE AT SEA

THE NATION

WORLD BROTHERHOOD

# The Large Circle

## THE CHURCH

*I was glad when they said unto me, Let us go into the house of the Lord.*

—Ps. 122:1

### PRAYER

In this hour of worship
　　Grant Thy presence, Lord!
Here, the world forgotten,
　　Feed us on Thy Word.
From our sins and sorrows
　　Here we seek release;
Of Thy love persuaded,
　　Find the path of peace.

—Author Unknown

### PRAYER ON ENTERING CHURCH

Heat and burden of the day
Help us, Lord, to put away.
Let no crowding, fretting cares
Keep earth-bound our spirit's prayers.
Carping criticism take
From our hearts for Jesus' sake,

*O send out thy light and thy truth: let them lead me; let them bring me unto thy holy hill, and to thy tabernacles.*　　—Ps. 43:3

In this little hour that we
Spend in fellowship with thee.
Search us, keenly, Lord, we pray
Lest we leave thy house today
Through our stubbornness unfed—
By the true and living bread—
Lest we know not that we thirst.
Selfishness that we have nursed
Through the years, O blessed Lord—
Smite it with thy two-edged sword.
Make us over! Make us kind.
Let no lonely stranger find
Lack of friendly handclasp, or
Pass unwelcomed through the door.
Let the whole week sweeter be
For this hour we spend with thee.
—BERTHA GERNEAUX WOODS

## SABBATH MORNING WORSHIP

Again, Dear Lord, we meet
  To worship in Thy name,
Teach us to sing Thy praise
  And spread abroad Thy fame.
Abide with us throughout this day,
Help us by faith to watch and pray.

Within these hallowed courts
  Reveal Thy wondrous grace,
Possess each restless heart
  And sanctify the place.
Abide with us in heavenly power
And glorify this sacred hour.

*How amiable are thy tabernacles, O Lord of hosts!*    —Ps. 84:1

May truth from out Thy word
   Break forth in light divine,
Cast out all doubt and fear
   And in the darkness shine.
Abide with us and ere we part
Illumine every troubled heart.

Reveal Thyself to us
   A great reality,
That we forevermore
   May live to honor Thee.
Abide with us in all our need,
Our hearts to cheer, our ways to lead.
          —DWIGHT EDWARDS MARVIN

## HYMN OF DEDICATION

Father, here a temple in Thy name we build;
Ever may Thy purpose in it be fulfilled.
Circled by Thy kindness, and Thy smile above,
May it stand for worship, service, faith and love.

Here may all who enter, feel Thy presence near,
Here the Holy Spirit bring a message clear.
Of Thy Son, beloved, child and youth be taught;
Measured by His standard, character be wrought.

May the sad find comfort, weary ones find rest,
Here the sick and lonely be with friendship blest;
Strength for those who falter, faith for all who doubt,
May Thy love, O Father, bind this place about.
          —ELIZABETH E. SCANTLEBURY

*Thy servant prayeth before thee to day: that thine eyes may be open toward this house night and day.*     —I Kings 8:28, 29

## DEDICATION

Thou, whose unmeasured temple stands,
    Built over earth and sea,
Accept the walls that human hands
    Have raised, O God, to Thee!

Lord, from Thine inmost glory send,
    Within these courts to bide,
The peace that dwelleth without end
    Serenely by Thy side!

May erring minds that worship here
    Be taught the better way;
And they who mourn, and they who fear,
    Be strengthened as they pray.

May faith grow firm, and love grow warm,
    And pure devotion rise,
While round these hallowed walls the storm
    Of earthborn passion dies.

        —WILLIAM CULLEN BRYANT

## DEDICATION

We dedicate a church today.
Lord Christ, I pray
Within the sound of its great bell
There is no mother who must hold
Her baby close against the cold—
So only have we served Thee well;

*Mine house shall be called an house of prayer for all people.*
        —Isa. 56:7

The wind blows sharp, the snow lies deep.
If we shall keep
Thy hungry ones, and sore distressed,
From pain and hardship, then may we
Know we have builded unto Thee,
And that each spire and arch is blest.

Lord Christ, grant we may consecrate
To Thee this church we dedicate.
—Ethel Arnold Tilden

## RALLYING HYMN FOR THE CHURCH

Lord, Thy power knows no declining,
   Thus, Thy many works declare;
Sun, moon, stars still keep their shining,
   There is order everywhere.
There are sacraments that tell us
   With Thy help we can prevail;
But alone, though e'er so zealous,
   We are weak and sure to fail.

Human need is all about us—
   Loads to lift, and tears to dry;
Evil forces seem to flout us,
   And our ranks stand helpless by.
Lord, to us the world is calling—
   Bidding us to right its wrong;
For around it now are falling
   Citadels it trusted long.

Holy Spirit, so inspire us,
   That our hearts may flame anew,
That each one may be desirous
   Something now worth-while to do.

*Not forsaking the assembling of ourselves together.* —Heb. 10:25

From our lethargy awake us,
    Link us to a great crusade;
In Thy service do Thou make us
    Happy, strong, and unafraid.
                        —ALEXANDER LOUIS FRASER


## GOD OF YEARS, THY LOVE HATH LED US
### Centennial Hymn—1837-1937

God of years, Thy love hath led us,
    Thou hast been our bulwark strong,
Wall of fire against the wicked,
    Sword of power against the wrong.
Thou hast blest of old Thy servants
    As they bore Thy message far;
We who follow in their footsteps
    Evermore their debtors are.


Onward lead, O King eternal,
    Lo, we heed Thy high command,
Bear good news to every people,
    Far and near, in every land.
Thine they are, Thy love doth seek them,
    Thou wouldst bring them to the light;
Lead us on till darkness brightens,
    On till faith is lost in sight.


Lead us forth, a Church united,
    Strong, courageous, in Thy might.
Lo, the fields are white with harvest,
    Sheaves to garner ere the night.


*The Lord is my rock, and my fortress, and my deliverer; my God, my strength, in whom I will trust.*                        —Ps. 18:2

One our purpose, One our Leader,
  Thus Thy Church shall never fail;
Lead us on, O King eternal,
  So shall love, world-wide, prevail.
                    —JAY GLOVER ELDRIDGE

## AT HIS TABLE

Our poor, doubting souls refresh!
Thou hast promised that Thy flesh
And Thy blood shall fill our need,
Being "meat and drink indeed."

So we dare to venture, Lord,
To approach this blessed board,
Sin-stained and with catching breath,
Take these symbols of Thy death.

Bless them to our use and strength,
Grant our wearied souls at length
Love's assurance, faith's increase,—
Thy past-understanding peace!
                    —BERTHA GERNEAUX WOODS

## IN REMEMBRANCE

In remembrance, Lord, I come
  Before Thy table spread,
Of Thy body pierced for me,
  Thy blood so freely shed.
Though unworthy, Lord, am I,
  Grant me Thy pardoning grace;
Take away the sin that hides
  From me Thy glorious face.

*And when he had given thanks, he brake it, and said, Take, eat; this is my body, which is broken for you.*          —I Cor. 11:24

87

Bless the sacred bread and cup
　　Of which I now partake;
Take my heart, 'tis all I have
　　To give for Thy sweet sake.
Break to me the bread of life
　　My hungry soul to feed;
Keep me close and true to Thee
　　'Til Thou return indeed.

—JULIA BENSON PARKER

# THE MINISTER

*Take heed to the ministry which thou hast received in the Lord,
that thou fulfil it.*

—Col. 4:17

## THE PARSON'S PRAYER

I do not ask
That crowds may throng the temple,
　　That standing room be priced;
I only ask that as I voice the message,
　　They may see Christ!

I do not ask
For churchly pomp or pageant,
　　Or music such as wealth alone can buy;
I only ask that as I voice the message,
　　He may be nigh!

I do not ask
That men may sound my praises
　　Or headlines spread my name abroad;
I only pray that as I voice the message,
　　Hearts may find God!

*Lo, I am with you alway.*　　　　　　　—Matt. 28:20

88

I do not ask
For earthly place or laurel,
  Or of this world's distinctions any part;
I only ask when I have voiced the message,
    My Saviour's heart!
                          —RALPH S. CUSHMAN


## A PASTOR'S PRAYER

Almighty God, may thoughts of Thee
  Fill all my mind and heart;
That as I seek to speak Thy Word,
  Naught else shall share a part.


I would be filled with power Divine,
  My feet on solid ground,
To boldly give Thy message forth
  With no uncertain sound.


May deeper knowledge of Thy will
  My daily portion be,
May Christ alone by word and deed,
  Be magnified in me.


And when we reach our Heavenly Home,
  With all the ransomed there;
May those I've loved and served while here,
  In all its glory share.
                          —GRACE E. TROY

*And he said unto me, My grace is sufficient for thee: for my strength is made perfect in weakness.  Most gladly therefore will I rather glory in my infirmities, that the power of Christ may rest upon me.*
                          —II COR. 12:9

## A WORKER'S PRAYER

Lord, speak to me, that I may speak
    In living echoes of thy tone;
As thou hast sought, so let me seek
    Thine erring children, lost and lone.

O lead me, Lord, that I may lead
    The wandering and the wavering feet;
O feed me, Lord, that I may feed
    Thy hungering ones with manna sweet.

O strengthen me, that while I stand
    Firm on the Rock and strong in thee,
I may stretch out a loving hand
    To wrestlers with the troubled sea.

O teach me, Lord, that I may teach
    The precious things thou dost impart;
And wing my words, that they may reach
    The hidden depths of many a heart.
        —FRANCES RIDLEY HAVERGAL

## THE SACRAMENT OF WORK

Christ,
For the men we pray
Before whom—in weakness and folly,
In emptiness, nothingness, shame—
We stand forth to-day, to tell them in word or in act of
    Thyself.

*Let a man so account of us, as of the ministers of Christ, and stewards
of the mysteries of God.*         —I Cor. 4:1

Christ,
Send forth in their hearts
The joyful triumphant might of Thy Spirit,
To show them Thy beauty,
To fill their souls with desire of Thyself.

Christ,
Hide us, hide us, Thy worthless and powerless tools,
And stand forth Thyself,
Calling Thine own, whom Thou lovest,
To high heroic achievement, to life for Thyself.

Christ,
May they see Thy beauty:
Christ,
May they fall in love with Thyself:
Christ,
May their souls be o'erwhelmed
With the deathless splendour of Thy free grace,
With yearning to live and to die for Thee,
To be held forever by Thee,
The brethren, the friends, the slaves of Thyself.

Christ,
Be manifest this day.

—J. S. Hoyland

## A MINISTER'S PRAYER

O God, help me proclaim Thy truth
To all who seek, old age or youth.
For me, I pray, the prophet's eye,

*I was not disobedient unto the heavenly vision.*　　—Acts 26:19

A voice like Aaron's ancient cry
Against the wrongs of every age;
Grant me the wisdom of the sage;
God, grant me grace in all my days
To counsel well Thy wondrous ways,
That I may sense Thy Spirit near
And walk with Thee, so that no fear
Shall dim Thy Truth nor stay Thy Voice,
'Til all shall hear Thee and rejoice!

—J. M. BEMISS

## A PASTOR'S PRAYER
## FOR HIS CONGREGATION

Lord, give Thy people hearing ears
    Who worship here today;
Obedient, may they follow Thee
    Along the narrow way.

May they be strengthened by Thy might,
    Built up in faith and love,
To fit them for life's service here
    And for their Home above.

Should sorrow be their portion, Lord,
    Oh, bring Thy comfort nigh.
In storm of trials, calm their fear
    And all their need supply.

And as they, Lord, receive from Thee
    Thy blessings, rich and free,

*And let us not be weary in well doing: for in due season we shall reap,*
*if we faint not.*                                    —Gal. 6:9

92

May they with glad and thankful hearts
   In all things yield to Thee.

          —GRACE E. TROY

# THE TEACHER

*For when for the time ye ought to be teachers, ye have need that one teach you.*

          —Heb. 5:12

## A PRAYER FOR TEACHERS

As to the seer in ancient time
   The angel came with coal aflame,
And touched his lips that he might speak,
   O God, in Thine almighty name,—
So to us in this later day
Send down a purifying ray.

Put forth Thy hand and touch our mouths—
   Whose holy task it is to teach
And guide the minds of eager youth,—
   That we may have inspiring speech.
Grant us vast patience, insight wise,
The open mind and heart and eyes.

Thus cleansed and quickened may we go
   And teach those in the morn of life
The beauty and the might of peace,

*Therefore, my beloved brethren, be ye stedfast, unmoveable, always abounding in the work of the Lord, forasmuch as ye know that your labour is not in vain in the Lord.*      —I Cor. 15:58

The sin and ugliness of strife.
Then shall the angel's voice proclaim,
"You, too, have spoken in God's name."
—MARGUERITE EMILIO

## THE TEACHER

Lord, who am I to teach the way
To little children day by day,
So prone myself to go astray?

I teach them Knowledge, but I know
How faint they flicker and how low
The candles of my knowledge glow.

I teach them Love for all mankind
And all God's creatures, but I find
My love comes lagging far behind.

Lord, if their guide I still must be,
Oh, let the little children see
A teacher leaning hard on Thee.
—LESLIE PINCKNEY HILL

## THE PRAYER OF A TEACHER

If I had seen Thee, Master,
    With children on Thy knee,
And heard Thy loving accents,
    "Let children come to Me,"

I think the inspiration
    Would last through all my days:

*Behold, God exalteth by his power: who teacheth like him?*
—Job 36:22

I'd speak—they'd follow after;
 They'd speak—I'd walk their ways.

O Master, fill my being
 With grace that comes from Thee:
And draw my little children
 Unto Thyself through me.
     —Elizabeth McE. Shields


## THE TEACHER'S PRAYER

My Lord, I do not ask to stand
 As king or prince of high degree.
I only pray that, hand in hand,
 A child and I may come to Thee.

Help me to share what Thou dost give
 And be a friend, a trusted guide.
As in Thy sight, oh, let me live.
 May selfishness be crucified.

Thou art the life, the truth, the way
 That leads to God, that saves from sin.
Oh, may my teaching, day by day,
 Help those in need, Thy life to win.

Oh, grant Thy patience, Lord, to share
 Thy holy purpose, life to bring.
May I the inexperience bear
 Of those who need love's fostering.
     —Norman E. Richardson

*Let him that is taught in the word communicate unto him that teacheth in all good things.*  —Gal. 6:6

## THE TEACHER'S PRAYER

O Lord of Life and God of Love,
    Make us to know, we ask,
The beauty of the trust we bear,
    The glory of our task!

Strengthen our hands and cleanse our hearts,
    Lighten our eyes, and make
Us worthy of our calling, for
    The children's Master's sake!

—NANCY BYRD TURNER

## LET ME GUIDE A LITTLE CHILD

Dear Lord, I do not ask
That Thou should'st give me some high work of Thine,
Some noble calling, or some wondrous task.

Give me a little hand to hold in mine;
Give me a little child to point the way
Over the strange, sweet path that leads to Thee;
Give me a little voice to teach to pray;
Give me two shining eyes Thy face to see.

The only crown I ask, dear Lord, to wear
Is this: That I may teach a little child.

I do not ask that I may ever stand
Among the wise, the worthy, or the great;
I only ask that softly, hand in hand,
A child and I may enter at the gate.

—AUTHOR UNKNOWN

*Commit thy way unto the Lord; trust also in him, and he shall bring it to pass.* —Ps. 37:5

# MISSIONS

*And he said unto them, Go ye into all the world, and preach the gospel to every creature.*

—Mark 16:15

## OUR MISSIONARIES

Forget them not, O Christ, who stand
Thy vanguard in the distant land!

In flood, in flame, in dark, in dread,
Sustain, we pray, each lifted head!

Be Thou in every faithful breast,
Be peace and happiness and rest!

Exalt them over every fear;
In peril, come Thyself more near!

Let heaven above their pathway pour
A radiance from its open door!

Turn Thou the hostile weapons, Lord,
Rebuke each wrathful alien horde!

Thine are the loved for whom we crave
That Thou wouldst keep them strong and brave.

Thine is the work they strive to do;
Their foes so many, they so few.

Yet Thou art with them and Thy Name
Forever lives, is aye the same.

*But ye shall receive power, after that the Holy Ghost is come upon you: and ye shall be witnesses unto me, both in Jerusalem, and in all Judaea, and in Samaria, and unto the uttermost part of the earth.*

—Acts 1:8

Thy conquering Name, O Lord, we pray.
Quench not its light in blood today!

Be with Thine own, Thy loved, who stand
Christ's vanguard in the storm-swept land!
—MARGARET E. SANGSTER

## PRAYER

Eternal God, whose power upholds
Both flower and flaming star,
To whom there is no here nor there,
No time, no near nor far,
No alien race, no foreign shore,
No child unsought, unknown:
O send us forth, Thy prophets true,
To make all lands Thine own!

O God of love, whose spirit wakes
In every human breast,
Whom love, and love alone can know,
In whom all hearts find rest:
Help us to spread Thy gracious reign
Till greed and hate shall cease,
And kindness dwell in human hearts,
And all the earth find peace!

O God of truth, whom science seeks
And reverent souls adore,
Who lightest every earnest mind
Of every clime and shore:
Dispel the gloom of error's night,
Of ignorance and fear,
Until true wisdom from above
Shall make life's pathway clear!

*And ye are witnesses of these things.*          —Luke 24:48

O God of beauty, oft revealed
   In dreams of human art,
In speech that flows to melody,
   In holiness of heart:
Teach us to ban all ugliness
   That blinds our eyes to Thee,
Till all shall know the loveliness
   Of lives made fair and free.

O God of righteousness and grace,
   Seen in the Christ, Thy Son,
Whose life and death reveal Thy face,
   By whom Thy will was done:
Inspire Thy heralds of good news
   To live Thy life divine,
Till Christ is formed in all mankind
   And every land is Thine!

—HENRY HALLAM TWEEDY

## SPREAD THE LIGHT

There is darkness still, gross darkness, Lord,
On this fair earth of Thine.
There are prisoners still in the prison-house,
Where never a light doth shine.
There are doors still bolted against Thee,
There are faces set like a wall;
And over them all the Shadow of Death
Hangs like a pall.
   *Do you hear the voices calling,*
   *Out there in the black of the night?*

*Then spake Jesus again unto them, saying, I am the light of the world: he that followeth me shall not walk in darkness, but shall have the light of life.* —John 8:12

*Do you hear the sobs of the women,*
*Who are barred from the blessed light?*
*And the children—the little children—*
*Do you hear their pitiful cry?*
*O, brothers, we must seek them,*
*Or there in the dark they die!*

Spread the Light!  Spread the Light!
Till earth's remotest bounds have heard
The glory of the Living Word;
Till those that see not have their sight;
Till all the fringes of the night
Are lifted, and the long-closed doors
Are wide for ever to the Light.
Spread—the—Light!

*O then shall dawn the golden days,*
*To which true hearts are pressing;*
*When earth's discordant strains shall blend—*
*The one true God confessing;*
*When Christly thought and Christly deed*
*Shall bind each heart and nation,*
*In one Grand Brotherhood of Men,*
*And one high consecration.*

—JOHN OXENHAM

## THE MISSIONARY

O matchless honor, all unsought,
High privilege, surpassing thought
That thou shouldst call us, Lord, to be
Linked in work-fellowship with thee!

*And I, if I be lifted up from the earth, will draw all men unto me.*
—John 12:32

To carry out *thy* wondrous plan,
To bear *thy* messages to man;
"In trust," with Christ's own word of grace
To every soul of human race.

—AUTHOR UNKNOWN

## A HOME MISSION PRAYER

Look from thy sphere of endless day,
    O God of mercy and of might;
In pity look on those who stray,
    Benighted, in this land of light.

In peopled vale, in lonely glen,
    In crowded mart, by stream or sea,
How many of the sons of men
    Hear not the message sent from thee!

Send forth thy heralds, Lord, to call
    The thoughtless young, the hardened old,
A scattered, homeless flock, till all
    Be gathered to thy peaceful fold.

Send them thy mighty word to speak,
    Till faith shall dawn, and doubt depart,
To awe the bold, to stay the weak,
    And bind and heal the broken heart.

Then all these wastes, a dreary scene,
    That make us sadden as we gaze,
Shall grow with living waters green,
    And lift to heaven the voice of praise.

—WILLIAM CULLEN BRYANT

*And they shall not teach every man his neighbour, and every man his*
*brother, saying, Know the Lord: for all shall know me, from the least*
*to the greatest.*     —Heb. 8:11

# THOSE WHO FLY

*He shall cover thee with his feathers, and under his wings shalt thou trust.*

—Ps. 91:4

## OUR AIRMEN

Gracious God, our Heavenly Father,
  Who dost Heaven and earth control,
Do Thou keep our fearless airmen—
  Speed them safely to their goal.

Perilous their great adventure
  Far above the mist and clouds,
Where the mighty eagle soareth,
  Where the tempest oft enshrouds.

Known to Thee their course, O Father,
  Whether over sea or land,
Thou who ledst by cloud and fire
  Guide them by Thine unseen Hand.

Heed their prayers, O gracious Father,
  Speak to every anxious heart,
Thou who formed the vast creation,
  Knowest compass, map, and chart.

As the darkness closes 'round them,
  As they speed on through the night,

*For he shall give his angels charge over thee, to keep thee in all thy ways.*
                                        —Ps. 91:11

Thou who slumberest not nor sleepest,
   Keep them, Father, in Thy sight.

God be with our gallant airmen!
   Many plaudits they have won.
May they reach the goal of Heaven
   There to hear Thee say, "Well done."
            —GERTRUDE ROBINSON DUGAN

## FOR THOSE WHO FLY

Great Father, hear our earnest prayer
For those who travel through the air,
Guide them whereso'er they go
And Thy blest presence let them know.
   Hear, oh, hear our earnest prayer
   For those who travel through the air!

As swiftly through the air they fly
Guard them with Thy watchful eye.
However far their flight may be,
Draw them ever nearer Thee.
   Hear, oh, hear our earnest prayer
   For all who travel through the air!

When storms are nigh and clouds are dark
Guide Thou the hand that steers their bark
Far above the land and sea
By day and night their Pilot be.
   Hear, oh, hear our earnest prayer
   For all who travel through the air!

*The angel of the Lord encampeth round about them that fear him,
and delivereth them.*            —Ps. 34:7

To their brave efforts lend Thine aid
And whisper low: "Be not afraid."
O'er mountain, valley, sea, and plain
Bring them safely home again.
    Hear, oh, hear our earnest prayer
    For all who travel through the air!
—ALICE B. JOYNES

## A PRAYER FOR AVIATORS

God of the sky, enthroned in azure blue,
    Lord of the air, who guides the wings at will,
God Thou the pilot as he journeys through
    High altitudes, o'er valley, plain, and hill.


God of the storm, whose majesty and power
    Are manifested in driving hail and rain,
Guard Thou the pilot in his crisis hour,
    Oh, bring him safely to a port again.


God of the night, whose darkness all enfolds,
    Hiding from view both landing field and course,
Give Thou safe guidance, as each beacon holds
    High shafts of light, with never-failing source.


God of our lives, we journey through the years,
    In joy and pain, teach us to trust Thy care!
In heights of bliss, in storms of doubts and fears,
    Show us our course and Thou wilt find us there.
—NORMAN E. RICHARDSON

*But be not thou far from me, O Lord.*    —Ps. 22:19

# THOSE AT SEA

*The Lord on high is mightier than the noise of many waters, yea, than the mighty waves of the sea.*

—Ps. 93:4

## ETERNAL FATHER, STRONG TO SAVE

Eternal Father, strong to save,
Whose arm doth bind the restless wave,
Who bidd'st the mighty ocean deep
Its own appointed limits keep:
O hear us when we cry to Thee
For those in peril on the sea.

O Saviour, whose almighty word
The winds and waves submissive heard,
Who walkedst on the foaming deep
And calm amid its rage didst sleep:
O hear us when we cry to Thee
For those in peril on the sea.

O sacred Spirit, who didst brood
Upon the chaos dark and rude,
Who bad'st its angry tumult cease,
And gavest light and life and peace:
O hear us when we cry to Thee
For those in peril on the sea.

O Trinity of love and power,
Our brethren shield in danger's hour;

*He maketh the storm a calm, so that the waves thereof are still.*

—Ps. 107:29

From rock and tempest, fire and foe,
Protect them wheresoe'er they go;
And ever let there rise to Thee
Glad hymns of praise from land and sea.

—WILLIAM WHITING

## A SEA-PRAYER

Lord of wind and water
　Where the ships go down
Reaching to the sunrise,
　Lifting like a crown,

Out of the deep-hidden
　Wells of night and day—
Mind the great sea-farers
　On the open way.

When the last lights darken
　On the far coastline,
Wave and port and peril,
　Yea,—Lord—all are Thine.

—WILLIAM STANLEY BRAITHWAITE

# THE NATION

*Blessed is the nation whose God is the Lord.*

—Ps. 33:12

## PRAYER FOR THE PRESIDENT

Lay Thou, O God, Thy quickening hand
Upon the ruler of our land.

*Remember them which have the rule over you.*　　—Heb. 13:7

Uphold his frame with sturdy might,
Flash on his brain revealing light.

Far may he move from party strife,
But closer to the people's life.

Touch Thou his soul with tenderness
To heed the farthest faint distress.

Embolden Thou his manly heart
Ever to play the patriot's part.

All men may he as brethren own,
Yet dare at need to stand alone.

As he is true to us, may we
Uphold him ever loyally.

As he is true to Thee, O God,
Protect him with Thy staff and rod.

Save him from coward hand and tongue,
Renew his soul, and keep him young.

And when his task is ended, then
Bestow Thy crowning praise. *Amen.*
—Amos R. Wells

## OUR COUNTRY

Dear God, our country needs Thee
To help and heal and bless,
To give the rulers wisdom,
To grant to right success,

*The Lord will give strength unto his people.* —Ps. 29:11

To feed her many millions,
　　To keep her always free,
To lead them in the way of Christ,
　　Where they may walk with Thee.
　　　　　　　　—AUTHOR UNKNOWN


## THE PEOPLE'S PRAYER

God bless our dear United States,
Preserve the land from evil fates,
Lift high her banner fair and free,
And guard her bounds from sea to sea.

From foe without and foe within,
From open shame and hidden sin,
From boastful pride and greedy store,
God keep our nation evermore.

Forever may her friendly hands
Receive the poor of other lands
In kindliness of sisterhood,
And fill their arms with ample good.

Assailed by battle hosts of wrong,
God help our country to be strong.
Assailed by falsehood's crafty crew,
God help our country to be true.

God hold the nation's aim sincere,
God save her heart from coward fear.
God prosper her in true success.
And crown her head with worthiness.

*Trust in him at all times; ye people, pour out your heart before him:*
*God is a refuge for us.*　　　　　　　　　　—Ps. 62:8

God bless our dear United States,
Preserve the land from evil fates,
Lift high her banner fair and free,
And ever guard her liberty.

—Amos R. Wells

## RECESSIONAL

God of our fathers, known of old,
  Lord of our far-flung battle-line,
Beneath whose awful Hand we hold
  Dominion over palm and pine—
Lord God of Hosts, be with us yet,
Lest we forget—lest we forget!

The tumult and the shouting dies;
  The captains and the kings depart:
Still stands Thine ancient sacrifice,
  An humble and a contrite heart.
Lord God of Hosts, be with us yet,
Lest we forget—lest we forget!

Far-called, our navies melt away;
  On dune and headland sinks the fire:
Lo, all our pomp of yesterday
  Is one with Nineveh and Tyre!
Judge of the Nations, spare us yet,
Lest we forget—lest we forget!

If, drunk with sight of power, we loose
  Wild tongues that have not Thee in awe.
Such boastings as the Gentiles use,
  Or lesser breeds without the Law—

*Righteousness exalteth a nation: but sin is a reproach to any people.*
—Prov. 14:34

Lord God of Hosts, be with us yet,
Lest we forget—lest we forget!

For heathen heart that puts her trust
　　In reeking tube and iron shard,
All valiant dust that builds on dust,
　　And guarding, calls not Thee to guard,
For frantic boast and foolish word—
Thy Mercy on Thy People, Lord!

　　　　　　　　　　—RUDYARD KIPLING

# WORLD BROTHERHOOD

*And many nations shall come, and say, Come, and let us go up
to the mountain of the Lord.*

　　　　　　　　　　—Micah 4:2

## SOUND THY TRUMPET, GOD OF ACTION

O Thou God who at creation
　　Looked on all Thy work as good,
Move the will of every nation,
　　At Thy call to brotherhood.
On the lap of all the ages,
　　Christ's great program long has lain,
Urged by martyrs, saints, and sages,
　　To assuage creation's pain.

From the dark, dim halls of mystery,
　　Where entombed lie nations' dead,
Comes the warning of their history,
　　As the years have onward sped;

*Behold, how good and how pleasant it is for brethren to dwell together
in unity!* 　　　　　　　　　—Ps. 133:1

That no people, though their story
   Sings of power, without, within,
Seeking only selfish glory,
   Immortality can win.

Sound Thy trumpet, God of action,
   O'er this wrangling, suffering world,
Till to nation, race, and faction,
   Thy great challenge has been hurled;
Till the mountain peaks ascending,
   Catch the glory of the morn
Of a peace, that shall unending
   Shine on nations yet unborn.

—ARTHUR B. DALE

## PRAYER FOR FAITH IN PEACE

From the gathered nations thrust
Every hindering thing—distrust,
Selfishness, and greed, and lust.

In our own heart—this our prayer—
For Thy blessed peace prepare,
Make us loving, make us care

For all peoples, greatest, least,
O our Shepherd, our High Priest,
Let there be no west, no east

In our thinking.  Hates and fears
Fostered through the bitter years,
Help the nations yield, with tears.

*He maketh wars to cease unto the end of the earth.*  —Ps. 46:9

No defeat, Lord, let us see
Looming up before us.  We
Have exhaustless stores in Thee.

Thine the will for peace indeed!
Faith, dear Lord, our greatest need—
Water Thou the mustard seed!
—BERTHA GERNEAUX WOODS

## PEACE

Peace in our time, O Lord,
To all the peoples—Peace!
Peace surely based upon Thy will
And built in righteousness.

Thy power alone can break
The fetters that enchain
The sorely stricken soul of life,
And make it live again.

Too long mistrust and fear
Have held our souls in thrall;
Sweep through the earth, keen breath of heaven,
And sound a nobler call!

Come, as Thou didst of old,
In love so great that men
Shall cast aside all other gods
And turn to Thee again!

Oh, shall we never learn
The truth all time has taught—
That without God as architect
Our building comes to naught?

*The earth shall be full of the knowledge of the Lord, as the waters
cover the sea.* —Isa. 11:9

Lord, help us, and inspire
Our hearts and lives, that we
May build, with all Thy wondrous gifts,
A Kingdom meet for Thee!

Peace in our time, O Lord,
To all the peoples—Peace!
Peace that shall crown a glad new world
With Thy High Sovereignties,
O Living Christ, who still
Dost all our burdens share,
Come now and reign within the hearts
Of all men everywhere!

—JOHN OXENHAM

## A PRAYER FOR PEACE

Dear Father, whom we cannot see,
We know that Thou art near;
With longing hearts we turn to Thee,
And ask that Thou wilt set us free
From war and hate and fear.

Dear Father, King of love and peace,
We know that Thou art strong;
Make conflicts everywhere to cease,
Let mercy everywhere increase,
And kindness conquer wrong.

Dear Father, Lord of sea and land,
We know that Thou art wise;
Oh, make the nations understand
That only by Thy guiding hand
Can splendid peace arise.

—JOHN OXENHAM

*They shall beat their swords into plowshares, and their spears into pruninghooks: nation shall not lift up sword against nation, neither shall they learn war any more.* —Isa. 2:4

# Discipleship

THE QUIET HOUR

THANKFULNESS

TRUST

SUBMISSION

DEDICATION

SERVICE

# Discipleship

## THE QUIET HOUR

*But they that wait upon the Lord shall renew their strength.*
*—Isa. 40:31*

### OPEN MY EYES

Open my eyes, dear Lord, that I may see
Each message that Thy Word would speak to me,
Lest, reading lightly, heedlessly, I miss
Some shining truth from Thee!   I beg for this,
Oh, blessed Holy Spirit, linger near!

I need Thy patient teaching, making clear
The things I see so dimly.   Dwell within
My heart that questions.   Keep me from the sin
Of unbelief, of willfullness.   Thy thought
Help me think after Thee!   I would be taught
Thy will, Thy ways, Thy plan for me to live,
And when I disappoint Thee, oh, forgive!
             *—BERTHA GERNEAUX WOODS*


### THE WORD OF GOD

Word of the ever-lasting God,
    Will of his glorious Son;
Without thee how could earth be trod,
    Or heaven itself be won?

*Open thou mine eyes, that I may behold wondrous things out of thy law.*                          *—Ps. 119:18*

Lord, grant us all aright to learn
 The wisdom it imparts;
And to its heavenly teaching turn,
 With simple, childlike hearts.

      —BERNARD BARTON

## HOME OF MY THOUGHTS

Be Thou
The home of my thoughts, dear Lord.
Like homing pigeons
Let them come
At day's tired end
To feed on Thy Word,
And find in Thee their rest,
Their home.

      —MARIE BARTON

## THY WORD IS LIKE A GARDEN, LORD

Thy Word is like a garden, Lord,
 With flowers bright and fair;
And every one who seeks may pluck
 A lovely cluster there.

Thy Word is like a deep, deep mine;
 And jewels rich and rare
Are hidden in its mighty depths
 For every searcher there.

Thy Word is like a starry host:
 A thousand rays of light
Are seen to guide the traveler,
 And make his pathway bright.

*The entrance of thy words giveth light.*  —Ps. 119:130

Thy Word is like an armory,
   Where soldiers may repair;
And find, for life's long battle-day,
   All needful weapons there.


O may I love Thy precious Word,
   May I explore the mine,
May I its fragrant flowers glean,
   May light upon me shine!

        —EDWIN HODDER


## PRAYER

God of the sunlight, God of the sea,
God of the twilight, God of the tree,
God of the midnight, God of the day,
God of the starlight, teach me to pray.

        —GRENVILLE KLEISER


## PRAYER

Lord, what a change within us one short hour
   Spent in Thy presence will prevail to make—
   What heavy burdens from our bosoms take,
What parchèd grounds refresh, as with a shower!
We kneel, and all around us seems to lower;
   We rise, and all, the distant and the near,
   Stand forth in sunny outline, brave and clear;
We kneel how weak, we rise how full of power!
Why, therefore, should we do ourselves this wrong,
Or others—that we are not always strong;

*He giveth power to the faint; and to them that have no might he
increaseth strength.*         —Isa. 40:29

That we are ever overborne with care;
  That we should ever weak or heartless be,
Anxious or troubled, when with us is prayer,
  And joy, and strength, and courage, are with Thee?

—R. C. TRENCH

## PRAYER

My God, is any hour so sweet,
  From blush of morn to evening star,
As that which calls me to thy feet:
  The hour of prayer?

Then is my strength by thee renewed;
  Then are my sins by thee forgiven;
Then dost thou cheer my solitude
  With hopes of heaven.

No words can tell what sweet relief
  Here for my every want I find;
What strength for warfare, balm for grief,
  What peace of mind.

—CHARLOTTE ELLIOTT

## BY THE WAY

### Luke 24:32

Go with me, Master, by the way,
  Make every day a walk with Thee;
New glory shall the sunshine gain,
  And all the clouds shall lightened be.
Go with me on life's dusty road
And help me bear the weary load.

*Commit thy way unto the Lord; trust also in him, and he shall bring it to pass.* —Ps. 37:5

Talk with me, Master, by the way;
  The voices of the world recede,
The shadows darken o'er the land—
  How poor am I, how great my need.
Speak to my heart disquieted
Till it shall lose its fear and dread.

Bide with me, Master, all the way,
  Though to my blinded eyes unknown;
So shall I feel a Presence near
  Where I had thought I walked alone.
And when, far spent, the days decline,
Break Thou the bread, dear Guest of mine!
               —ANNIE JOHNSON FLINT

## MY PRAYER

Lord Jesus, make Thyself to me
A living, bright reality;
More present to faith's vision keen
Than any outward object seen;
More dear, more intimately nigh
Than e'en the sweetest earthly tie.
               —AUTHOR UNKNOWN

## THE FELLOWSHIP OF PRAYER

O Son of Man, who walked each day
  A humble road, serene and strong,
Go with me now upon life's way,
  My Comrade all the journey long.

*Did not our heart burn within us, while he talked with us by the way?*
               —Luke 24:32

So shall I walk in happiness,
  So shall my task with love be fraught—
If thou art near to mark and bless
  The labor done, the beauty wrought.

O Son of God, who came and shed
  A light for all the ages long,
Thy company shall make me glad,
  Thy fellowship shall keep me strong.

—NANCY BYRD TURNER

# THANKFULNESS

*Continue in prayer, and watch in the same with thanksgiving.*
—Col. 4:2

### A THANKFUL HEART

We thank Thee, Heavenly Father,
  For every earthly good.
For life, for health, for shelter,
  And for our daily food.

Oh, give us hearts to thank Thee
  For every blessing sent,
And whatsoe'er Thou sendest,
  Make us therewith content.

—AUTHOR UNKNOWN

### THANKSGIVING

Lord, I am thankful for this day
That gave me both of work and play;

*The Lord hath done great things for us; whereof we are glad.*
—Ps. 126:3

A sun-drenched sky, a scented breeze,
A healthy mind, a heart at ease.
Today a woman spoke to me
In words that make love's melody;
Today the handclasp of a friend
Gave life a holier, happier blend.
Dear Lord, believe me when I say
That I am thankful for this day.

—WHITNEY MONTGOMERY

## FATHER, WE THANK THEE

For flowers that bloom about our feet,
    Father, we thank Thee,
For tender grass so fresh and sweet,
    Father, we thank Thee,
For song of bird and hum of bee,
For all things fair we hear or see,
    Father in heaven, we thank Thee.

For blue of stream and blue of sky,
    Father, we thank Thee,
For pleasant shade of branches high,
    Father, we thank Thee,
For fragrant air and cooling breeze,
For beauty of the blooming trees,
    Father in heaven, we thank Thee.

For this new morning with its light,
    Father, we thank Thee,
For rest and shelter of the night,
    Father, we thank Thee,

*Now therefore, our God, we thank thee, and praise thy glorious name.*
                    —I Chron. 29:13

For health and food, for love and friends,
For everything Thy goodness sends,
    Father in heaven, we thank Thee.
                        —Author Unknown


## OUR PRAYER

Thou that hast given so much to me,
Give one thing more—a grateful heart;
Not thankful when it pleaseth me,
As if Thy blessings had spare days;
But such a heart, whose pulse may be
Thy praise.
                        —George Herbert


## THANKFULNESS

My God, I thank Thee who hast made
    The Earth so bright;
So full of splendor and of joy,
    Beauty and light;
So many glorious things are here,
    Noble and right!

I thank Thee, too, that Thou hast made
    Joy to abound;
So many gentle thoughts and deeds
    Circling us round,
That in the darkest spot of Earth
    Some love is found.

I thank Thee more that all our joy
    Is touched with pain;

*Let us come before his presence with thanksgiving.*    —Ps. 95:2

That shadows fall on brightest hours;
    That thorns remain;
So that Earth's bliss may be our guide,
    And not our chain.

I thank Thee, Lord, that Thou hast kept
    The best in store;
We have enough, yet not too much
    To long for more:
A yearning for a deeper peace,
    Not known before.

I thank Thee, Lord, that here our souls,
    Though amply blest,
Can never find, although they seek,
    A perfect rest,—
Nor ever shall, until they lean
    On Jesus' breast!

—ADELAIDE ANNE PROCTER

## THE UNDISCOVERED COUNTRY

Lord, for the erring thought
Not unto evil wrought:
Lord, for the wicked will
Betrayed and baffled still:
For the heart from itself kept,
Our thanksgiving accept.
For ignorant hopes that were
Broken to our blind prayer:
For pain, death, sorrow sent
Unto our chastisement:
For all loss of seeming good,
Quicken our gratitude.

—WILLIAM DEAN HOWELLS

*Sing unto the Lord with thanksgiving.*          —Ps. 147:7

## THANKSGIVING FOR BENEFITS RECEIVED

So often, Lord, I come to Thee
   To ask Thy help in stress,
But now in gratitude I come,
   To say my thankfulness;

For all the mercy Thou hast shown,
   In countless gracious ways,
I now would be of service, too,
   That I might prove my praise;

Lord, I would have a listening ear,
   To hear Thy children call,
In my own heart remembering,
   No need to Thee is small.

          —Lois Givens Vaughan

## THE THINGS I MISS

An easy thing, O Power Divine,
To thank Thee for these gifts of Thine!
For summer's sunshine, winter's snow,
For hearts that kindle, thoughts that glow.
But when shall I attain to this:
To thank Thee for the things I miss?

For all young Fancy's early gleams,
The dreamed-of joys that still are dreams,
Hopes unfulfilled, and pleasures known
Through others' fortunes, not my own,
And blessings seen that are not given,
And never will be, this side of heaven.

*And let the peace of God rule in your hearts, . . . . and be ye thankful.*    —Col. 3:15

Had I, too, shared the joys I see,
Would there have been a heaven for me?
Could I have felt Thy presence near
Had I possessed what I held dear?
My deepest fortune, highest bliss,
Have grown perchance from things I miss.

Sometimes there comes an hour of calm;
Grief turns to blessing, pain to balm;
A Power that works above my will
Still leads me onward, upward still;
And then my heart attains to this:
To thank Thee for the things I miss.
—THOMAS WENTWORTH HIGGINSON


## AT ALL TIMES

"I will bless the Lord at all times."—Psalm 34:1

I bless Thee for the devious ways
By which Thy grace has been made known;
For rich unfoldings of Thy mind,
For gracious help Thy hand hath known.

I bless Thee for the darkness, Lord—
The hours of keenest testing sore,
For always have I proved Thy word,
And learned to trust Thee more and more.

I bless Thee for the quiet hours,
The calm that held my vessel still
When feverish haste would drive me on—
I learned the sweetness of Thy will.

*Enter into his gates with thanksgiving, and into his courts with praise:*
*be thankful unto him, and bless his name.* —Ps. 100:4

I bless Thee for the lonely hours,
  The watches in the desert drear;
For ever closer hast Thou been
  When seem'st that no one else was near.

I bless Thee all times, precious Lord,
  Never an hour I do not prove
The sweetness of Thy tender grace,
  The greatness of Thy mighty love.
                              —ALICE REYNOLDS FLOWER

## UNANSWERED PRAYER

I thank Thee, Lord, for mine unanswered prayers,
  Unanswered save Thy quiet, kindly "Nay,"
Yet it seemed hard among my heavy cares
  That bitter day.

I wanted joy; but Thou didst know for me
  That sorrow was the gift I needed most,
And in its mystic depth I learned to see
  The Holy Ghost.

I wanted health; but Thou didst bid me sound
  The secret treasuries of pain,
And in the moans and groans my heart oft found
  Thy Christ again.

I wanted wealth; 'twas not the better part,
  There is a wealth with poverty oft given,
And Thou didst teach me of the gold of heart,
  Best gift of heaven.

*Bless the Lord, O my soul, and forget not all his benefits.*
                              —Ps. 103:2

I thank Thee, Lord, for these unanswered prayers,
   And for Thy word, the quiet, kindly "Nay."
'Twas Thy withholding lightened all my cares
   That blessed day.

—OLIVER HUCKEL

## AN AGED COUPLE GIVES THANKS

We thank Thee, Lord, for strength to serve,
And as we safely round this curve

In the long roadway of our years,
We thank Thee for more smiles than tears;

And for comforts here and joys to be
In the Heavenly Home someday with Thee;

We thank Thee for a faith that sees
Thy hand in all life's mysteries;

We thank Thee, Lord, and ask Thy grace
To serve Thee still throughout life's race.

We praise Thee for Thy Son who came,
And make our prayer in His dear name.

—LOIS GIVENS VAUGHAN

*Every good gift and every perfect gift is from above, and cometh down from the Father of lights, with whom is no variableness, neither shadow of turning.*    —Jas. 1:17

# TRUST

*Trust in him at all times; ye people, pour out your heart before him: God is a refuge for us.*

—Ps. 62:8

## HYMN OF TRUST

O Love Divine, that stooped to share
    Our sharpest pang, our bitterest tear,
On Thee we cast each earth-born care,
    We smile at pain while Thou art near!

Though long the weary way we tread,
    And sorrow crown each lingering year,
No path we shun, no darkness dread,
    Our hearts still whispering, Thou art near!

When drooping pleasure turns to grief,
    And trembling faith is changed to fear,
The murmuring wind, the quivering leaf,
    Shall softly tell us, Thou art near!

On Thee we fling our burdening woe,
    O Love Divine, forever dear,
Content to suffer while we know,
    Living and dying, Thou art near!

—Oliver Wendell Holmes

## VOYAGERS

O Maker of the Mighty Deep
    Whereon our vessels fare,

*In God have I put my trust: I will not be afraid what man can do unto me.*
    —Ps. 56:11

Above our life's adventure keep
   Thy faithful watch and care.
In Thee we trust, whate'er befall;
Thy sea is great, our boats are small.

We know not where the secret tides
   Will help us or delay,
Nor where the lurking tempest hides,
   Nor where the fogs are gray.
We trust in Thee, whate'er befall;
Thy sea is great, our boats are small.

When outward bound we boldly sail
   And leave the friendly shore,
Let not our heart of courage fail
   Until the voyage is o'er.
We trust in Thee, whate'er befall;
Thy sea is great, our boats are small.

When homeward bound we gladly turn,
   O bring us safely there,
Where harbor-lights of friendship burn
   And peace is in the air.
We trust in Thee, whate'er befall;
Thy sea is great, our boats are small.

Beyond the circle of the sea,
   When voyaging is past,
We seek our final port in Thee;
   O bring us home at last.
In Thee we trust, whate'er befall;
Thy sea is great, our boats are small.

           —HENRY VAN DYKE

*I will trust, and not be afraid.*        —Isa. 12:2

## "MY GRACE IS SUFFICIENT FOR THEE"

When, sin-stricken, burdened, and weary,
    From bondage I longed to be free,
There came to my heart the sweet message:
    "My grace is sufficient for thee."

Though tempted and sadly discouraged,
    My soul to this refuge will flee,
And rest in the blessed assurance:
    "My grace is sufficient for thee."

My bark may be tossed by the tempest
    That sweeps o'er the turbulent sea—
A rainbow illumines the darkness:
    "My grace is sufficient for thee."

O Lord, I would press on with courage,
    Though rugged the pathway may be,
Sustained and upheld by the promise:
    "My grace is sufficient for thee."

Soon, soon will the warfare be over,
    My Lord face to face I shall see,
And prove, as I dwell in His presence:
    "His grace was sufficient for me."

—Author Unknown


## MY TIMES ARE IN THY HAND

"My times are in thy hand";
    My God, I wish them there;

*Thy right hand upholdeth me.*                    —Ps. 63:8

132

My life, my friends, my soul, I leave
   Entirely to thy care.

"My times are in thy hand";
   Why should I doubt or fear?
A Father's hand will never cause
   His child a needless tear.
—WILLIAM F. LLOYD

## THE CHRISTIAN LIFE

I look to Thee in ev'ry need,
   And never look in vain;
I feel Thy strong and tender love,
   And all is well again;
The thought of Thee is mightier far
Than sin and pain and sorrow are.

Discouraged in the work of life,
   Disheartened by its load,
Shamed by its failures or its fears,
   I sink beside the road;
But let me only think of Thee,
And then new heart springs up in me.
—SAMUEL LONGFELLOW

# SUBMISSION

*Thy kingdom come. Thy will be done in earth, as it is in heaven.*

—Matt. 6:10

## MY JESUS, AS THOU WILT

My Jesus, as Thou wilt!
   O may Thy will be mine!

*When he hath tried me, I shall come forth as gold.*   —Job 23:10

Into Thy hand of love
I would my all resign.

Through sorrow or through joy,
Conduct me as Thine own;
And help me still to say,
"My Lord, Thy will be done."

—Benjamin Schmolck

## MY PRAYER

I kneel to pray,
But know not what to say:
I cannot tell
What may be ill or well:
But as I look
Into Thy Face or Book
I see a love
From which I cannot move:
And learn to rest
In this—Thy will is best:

Therefore I pray
Only have Thine own way
In everything
My all wise God and King.
Grant me the grace
In all to give Thee place:
This liberty
Alone I ask of Thee:
This only gift,
Have Thy way perfectly.

—Mark Guy Pearse

*I delight to do thy will, O my God.* —Ps. 40:8

134

## NOT MY WILL

Not my will though weary the way,
Not my will but Thine day by day:
Not self but the Saviour shall guide
And bring us at last to His side.

Not my will, when burdens press down,
Not my will, with foes all around;
But resting on infinite love,
All then will be made clear above.

Not my will when loved ones go "Home,"
Not my will when hearts are left lone:
For He knows our way from its dawn,
Out into the eternal morn.

Not my will but Thy will be done,
Not my will but Thine, Blessed Son.
  In the land of our rest
   We shall know it was best,
Not my will, but Thy will be done.

—GREEN FOREST

## "THY WILL BE DONE"

My God, my Father, while I stray
Far from my home, on life's rough way,
O teach me from my heart to say,
  "Thy will be done!"

*Father, if thou be willing, remove this cup from me: nevertheless, not my will, but thine, be done.*    —Luke 22:42

135

Renew my will from day to day;
Blend it with Thine, and take away
All that now makes it hard to say,
   "Thy will be done!"

Then, when on earth I breathe no more
The prayer oft mixed with tears before,
I'll sing upon a happier shore,
   "Thy will be done!"
                —CHARLOTTE ELLIOTT

## THY WILL BE DONE

Thy will be done, our Father,
  We kneel and humbly pray;
Oh, give to us the patience,
  That, in Thy time and way,
    "Thy will be done."

Give us the courage, Father,
  To say with purpose true,
E'en while life's angry billows
  May hide Thee from our view,
    "Thy will be done."

Though there be none to comfort
  In time of testing sore;
Oh, may we hear Thee, Saviour,
  Whisper the sweet words o'er,
    "Thy will be done."

Knowing no earthly trial
  Can with our Lord's compare,
Help us to say, our Father,
  From 'neath the cross we bear,
    "Thy will be done."
              —ANNA NORMAN OATES

*Teach me to do thy will; for thou art my God.*   —Ps. 143:10

## FULFIL THY WILL

O Lord, fulfil Thy Will
Be the days few or many, good or ill:
Prolong them, to suffice
For offering up ourselves Thy sacrifice;
Shorten them if Thou wilt,
To make in righteousness an end of guilt.
Yea, they will not be long
To souls who learn to sing a patient song:
Yea, short they will not be
To souls on tiptoe to flee home to Thee.
O Lord, fulfil Thy Will.
Make Thy will ours, and keep us patient still
Be the days few or many, good or ill.

—CHRISTINA G. ROSSETTI

## THE SACRIFICE OF THE WILL

Laid on thine altar, O my Lord Divine,
  Accept my will this day, for Jesus' sake;
I have no jewels to adorn thy shrine—
  Nor any world-proud sacrifice to make;
But here I bring within my trembling hand,
  This will of mine—a thing that seemeth small,
But Thou alone, O God, canst understand
  How, when I yield Thee this, I yield mine all.
Hidden therein, thy searching gaze can see
  Struggles of passion—visions of delight—
All that I love, and am, and fain would be,
  Deep loves, fond hopes, and longings infinite.
It hath been wet with tears and dimmed with sighs,
  Clinched in my grasp, till beauty hath it none—

*He died for all, that they which live should not henceforth live unto*
*themselves, but unto him which died for them, and rose again.*

                      —II. Cor. 5:15

Now, from thy footstool where it vanquished lies,
    The prayer ascendeth, "May thy will be done."
Take it, O Father, ere my courage fail,
    And merge it so in thine own Will, that e'en
If, in some desperate hour, my cries prevail,
    And thou give back my will, it may have been
So changed, so purified, so fair have grown,
    So one with thee, so filled with peace divine,
I may not see nor know it as my own,
    But, gaining back my will, may find it thine.

—AUTHOR UNKNOWN


## GOD'S WAY

Thy way, not mine, O Lord!
    However dark it be;
Lead me by Thine own hand,
    Choose out the path for me.

Smooth let it be, or rough,
    It will be still the best;
Winding or straight it matters not,
    It leads me to Thy rest.

I dare not choose my lot,
    I would not, if I might;
Choose Thou for me, O God!
    So shall I walk aright.

The kingdom that I seek
    Is Thine; so let the way
That leads to it be Thine;
    Else I must surely stray.

*And the Lord shall guide thee continually.*          —Isa. 58:11

Take Thou my cup, and it
  With joy or sorrow fill;
As best to Thee may seem;
  Choose Thou my good or ill.

Choose Thou for me my friends
  My sickness or my health;
Choose Thou my cares for me,
  My poverty or wealth.

Not mine, not mine the choice
  In things or great or small;
Be Thou my guide, my strength,
  My wisdom and my all.

—Horatius Bonar

# DEDICATION

*But we will give ourselves continually to prayer and to the ministry of the word.*

—Acts 6:4

Take my heart! for I cannot give it Thee:
Keep it! for I cannot keep it for Thee.

—St. Augustine

## TAKE MY LIFE

Take my life, and let it be
Consecrated, Lord, to Thee.
Take my moments and my days;
Let them flow in ceaseless praise.

*Let this mind be in you, which was also in Christ Jesus.*—Phil. 2:5

Take my hands, and let them move
At the impulse of Thy love.
Take my feet, and let them be
Swift and beautiful for Thee.

Take my voice, and let me sing,
Always, only, for my King.
Take my lips, and let them be
Filled with messages from Thee.
Take my silver and my gold;
Not a mite would I withhold.
Take my intellect, and use
Every power as Thou shalt choose.

Take my will, and make it Thine;
It shall be no longer mine.
Take my heart, it is Thine own;
It shall be Thy royal throne.
Take my love; my Lord, I pour
At Thy feet its treasure-store.
Take myself, and I will be
Ever, only, all for Thee.

—FRANCES RIDLEY HAVERGAL

## A COVENANT

Now, Lord, I give myself to Thee;
  I would be wholly Thine,
As Thou hast given Thyself to me,
  And Thou art wholly mine.
Oh, take me, seal me as Thine own,
Thine altogether—Thine alone!

—FRANCES RIDLEY HAVERGAL

*And ye shall seek me, and find me, when ye shall search for me with all your heart.*
—Jer. 29:13

## THINE

Thine, most gracious Lord,
 O make me wholly Thine—
Thine in thought, in word, and deed,
 For Thou, O Christ, art mine.


Thine, Lord, wholly Thine,
 Forever one with Thee—
Rooted, grounded in Thy love,
 Abiding, sure and free.

—ANNIE S. HAWKS


## SPIRIT OF GOD

Spirit of God, descend upon my heart;
 Wean it from earth; through all its pulses move;
Stoop to my weakness, mighty as Thou art,
 And make me love Thee as I ought to love.


Teach me to feel that Thou art always nigh;
 Teach me the struggles of the soul to bear,
To check the rising doubt, the rebel sigh;
 Teach me the patience of unanswered prayer.


Teach me to love Thee as Thine angels love,
 One holy passion filling all my frame;
The kindling of the heaven-descended Dove,
 My heart an altar, and Thy love the flame.

—GEORGE CROLY


*But the Comforter, . . . . the Holy Ghost, . . . . shall teach you
all things.* —John 14:26

## O HOLY GHOST, ARISE

O Holy Ghost, arise
   Thy temple fill:
With cleansing fire baptize
   My yielded will.

Breath from above, refine
   My waiting heart:
Impulse and power divine
   To me impart.

Thou very Light of Light,
   Poured from on high,
Kindle with vision bright
   My inward eye.

Cleanse, and illume, and fill—
   It shall be so:
Then send me where Thou will
   And I will go.

—A. J. GORDON

## A PRAYER

O that mine eyes might closèd be
To what concerns me not to see;
That deafness might possess mine ear
To what concerns me not to hear;
That truth my tongue might always tie
From ever speaking foolishly;

*If ye then, being evil, know how to give good gifts unto your children; how much more shall your heavenly Father give the Holy Spirit to them that ask him?* —Luke 11:13

That no vain thought might ever rest
Or be conceived within my breast;
That by each deed and word and thought
Glory may to my God be brought.
But what are wishes!  Lord, mine eye
On Thee is fixed; to Thee I cry!
Wash, Lord, and purify my heart,
And make it clean in every part;
And when 'tis clean, Lord, keep it, too,
For that is more than I can do.

—THOMAS ELLWOOD


## TEACH ME TO LIVE

Teach me to live!  'Tis easier far to die—
   Gently and silently to pass away—
On earth's long night to close the heavy eye,
   And waken in the glorious realms of day.

Teach me that harder lesson—how to live
   To serve Thee in the darkest paths of life.
Arm me for conflict, now fresh vigor give,
   And make me more than conqu'ror in the strife.

—AUTHOR UNKNOWN


## THY WILL BE DONE

Draw Thou my soul, O Christ,
   Closer to Thine;
Breathe into every wish
   Thy will divine!

*Moreover, it is required in stewards, that a man be found faithful.*
—I Cor. 4:2

Raise my low self above,
Won by Thy deathless love;
 Ever, O Christ, through mine
 Let Thy life shine.

Lead forth my soul, O Christ,
 One with Thine own,
Joyful to follow Thee
 Through paths unknown!
In Thee my strength renew;
Give me my work to do!
 Through me Thy truth be shown,
 Thy love made known.

       —LUCY LARCOM

# SERVICE

*For even the Son of man came not to be ministered unto, but to minister, and to give his life a ransom for many.*
       —Mark 10:45

## NOT TO BE MINISTERED TO

O Lord, I pray
That for this day
I may not swerve
By foot or hand
From Thy command
Not to be served, but to serve.

This, too, I pray,
That from this day

*Let your light so shine before men, that they may see your good works, and glorify your Father which is in heaven.*  —Matt. 5:16

No love of ease
  Nor pride prevent
  My good intent
Not to be pleased, but to please.

  And if I may,
  I'd have this day
Strength from above
  To set my heart
  In heavenly art
Not to be loved, but to love.

        —MALTBIE D. BABCOCK

## HERE AM I

I ask no heaven till earth be Thine;
No glory crown while work of mine
  Remaineth here.

When earth shall shine among the stars,
Her sins wiped out, her captives free,
Her voice a music unto Thee,
For crown, more work give Thou to me,
  Lord, here am I.

        —AUTHOR UNKNOWN

## O MASTER, LET ME WALK WITH THEE

O Master, let me walk with thee
In lowly paths of service free;
Tell me thy secret; help me bear
The strain of toil, the fret of care.

*Also I heard the voice of the Lord, saying, Whom shall I send, and who will go for us? Then said I, Here am I; send me.*—Isa. 6:8

Help me the slow of heart to move
By some clear, winning word of love;
Teach me the wayward feet to stay
And guide them in the homeward way.

Teach me thy patience; still with thee
In closer, dearer company,
In work that keeps faith sweet and strong,
In trust that triumphs over wrong;

In hope that sends a shining ray
Far down the future's broadening way;
In peace that only thou canst give,—
With thee, O Master, let me live!
—WASHINGTON GLADDEN

## MY DAILY PRAYER

If I can do some good today,
If I can serve along life's way,
If I can something helpful say,
Lord, show me how.

If I can right a human wrong,
If I can help to make one strong,
If I can cheer with smile or song,
Lord, show me how.

If I can aid one in distress,
If I can make a burden less,
If I can spread more happiness,
Lord, show me how.
—GRENVILLE KLEISER

*Therefore, my beloved brethren, be ye stedfast, unmoveable, always abounding in the work of the Lord, forasmuch as ye know that your labour is not in vain in the Lord.* —I Cor. 15:58

## PRAYER

Father, I scarcely dare to pray,
  So clear I see, now it is done,
That I have wasted half my day,
  And left my work but just begun.

So clear I see that things I thought
  Were right or harmless were a sin;
So clear I see that I have sought,
  Unconscious, selfish aims to win.

So clear I see that I have hurt
  The souls I might have helped to save;
That I have slothful been, inert,
  Deaf to the calls Thy leaders gave.

In outskirts of Thy kingdom vast,
  Father, the humblest spot give me;
Set me the lowliest task Thou hast;
  Let me, repentant, work for Thee!

—HELEN HUNT JACKSON

## A PRAYER

Grant me, O Lord, this day to see
The need this world may have for me;
    To play the friend
    Unto the end;
To bear my burden and to keep
My courage, though the way be steep.

*Not every one that saith unto me, Lord, Lord, shall enter into the
kingdom of heaven; but he that doeth the will of my Father which is
in heaven.*
                                        —Matt. 7:21

147

Grant me, O Lord, to set aside
The petty things of selfish pride;
    To toil without
    Too much of doubt;
To meet what comes of good or ill
And be a gracious neighbor, still.

Grant me, O Lord, to face the rain
And not too bitterly complain;
    Nor let a joy
    My calm destroy;
But teach me so to live that I
Can brother with each passer-by.
            —EDGAR A. GUEST

## A PRAYER POEM

O Master of the loving heart,
  The Friend of all in need,
We pray that we may be like Thee
  In thought and word and deed.

Thy days were full of kindly acts;
  Thy speech was true and plain;
And no one ever sought Thee, Lord,
  Or came to Thee in vain.

Thy hand was warm with sympathy;
  Thy hand God's strength revealed;
Who saw Thy face or felt Thy touch
  Were comforted and healed.

*So will I sing praise unto thy name for ever, that I may daily perform my vows.*
            —Ps. 61:8

O grant us hearts like Thine, dear Lord;
So joyous, true, and free
That all Thy children everywhere
Be drawn by us to Thee.

—CALVIN W. LAUFER

## MAKE ME KIND

God make me kind!
So many hearts are breaking,
And many more are aching
To hear the tender word.
God make me kind!
For I myself am learning
That my sad heart is yearning
For some sweet word to heal my hurt.
O Lord, do make me kind.

God make me kind!
So many hearts are needing
The balm to stop the bleeding
That my kind words can bring.
God make me kind!
For I am also seeking
The cure in someone's keeping
They should impart to my sick heart.
O Lord, do make me kind.

—DUNCAN McNEIL

## RADIO PRAYER

Dear Lord;
Let all the words
Speeding so swiftly through the air

*And be ye kind one to another.*          —Eph. 4:32

Be clear as light, and let each bear
Silvery joy such as the rare
Sweet notes of birds
Accord.

Wilt Thou
Let music find
The shadows that are dark with pain
And tears; let some soft lyric strain
Bring cheer and sunlight there again;
Let peace a mind
Endow.

I pray
That to the soul
Discouraged with long tasks undone,
Bright, gallant words may swiftly run,
Stirring his heart to valor, so that none
Shall miss his goal
Today.

—LEXIE DEAN ROBERTSON

## A NURSE'S PRAYER

Because the day that stretches out for me
Is full of busy hours, I come to Thee
To ask Thee, Lord, that Thou wilt see me through
The many things that I may have to do.
Help me to make more tempting every tray.
Help me to sense when pain must have relief.
Help me to deal with those borne down by grief.
Help me to take to every patient's room
The Light of Life to brighten up the gloom.

*A word fitly spoken is like apples of gold in pictures of silver.*
—Prov. 25:11

Help me to bring to every soul in fear
The sure and steadfast thought that Thou art near.
And if today, or if tonight, maybe,
Some patients in my care set out to sea
To face the great adventure we call death,
Sustain them, Father, in their parting breath.
Help me to live throughout this livelong day
As one who loves Thee well, dear Lord, I pray;
And when the day is done, and evening stars
Shine through the dark above the sunset bars,
When weary quite, I turn to seek my rest,
Lord, may I truly know I've done my best.

—RUTH WINANT WHEELER


## A PRAYER

Teach me, Father, how to go
Softly as the grasses grow;
Hush my soul to meet the shock
Of the wild world as a rock;
But my spirit, propt with power,
Make as simple as a flower.
Let the dry heart fill its cup,
Like a poppy looking up;
Let life lightly wear her crown,
Like a poppy looking down,
When its heart is filled with dew,
And its life begins anew.

Teach me, Father, how to be
Kind and patient as a tree.


*I beseech you therefore, brethren, by the mercies of God, that ye present your bodies a living sacrifice, holy, acceptable unto God.*

—Rom. 12:1

Joyfully the crickets croon
Under shady oak at noon;
Beetle, on his mission bent,
Tarries in that cooling tent.
Let me, also, cheer a spot,
Hidden field or garden grot—
Place where passing souls can rest
On the way and be their best.

—EDWIN MARKHAM

# The Soul's Needs

FORGIVENESS

FAITH

COURAGE

SUSTAINING POWER

COMFORT

# The Soul's Needs

## FORGIVENESS

*If thou, Lord, shouldest mark iniquities, O Lord, who shall stand?*
*But there is forgiveness with thee.*

—Ps. 130:3-4

### FORGIVENESS

When at Thy footstool, Lord, I bend,
　And plead with Thee for mercy there,
Think of the sinner's dying Friend,
　And for His sake receive my prayer!
Oh, think not of my shame and guilt,
　My thousand stains of deepest dye!
Think of the blood which Jesus spilt,
　And let that blood my pardon buy!

—HENRY FRANCIS LYTE

### A PRAYER

Lord, in mercy pardon me
　All that I this day have done:
Sins of every kind 'gainst Thee,
　Oh, forgive them, through Thy Son.

Make me, Jesus, like to Thee,
　Gentle, holy, meek, and mild,
My transgressions pardon me,
　Oh, forgive a sinful child.

—FRANCES RIDLEY HAVERGAL

*His merciful kindness is great toward us.*　　　—Ps. 117:2

155

## PSALM FIFTY-ONE

Show pity, Lord; O Lord, forgive;
Let a repenting rebel live;
Are not Thy mercies large and free?
May not a sinner trust in Thee?

My crimes are great, but don't surpass
The power and glory of Thy grace;
Great God, Thy nature hath no bound,
So let Thy pardoning love be found.

Oh, wash my soul from every sin,
And make my guilty conscience clean;
Here on my heart the burden lies,
And past offences pain mine eyes.

My lips with shame my sins confess,
Against Thy law, against Thy grace;
Lord, should Thy judgments grow severe,
I am condemned, but Thou art clear.

Should sudden vengeance seize my breath,
I must pronounce Thee just in death;
And if my soul were sent to hell,
Thy righteous law approves it well.

Yet save a trembling sinner, Lord,
Whose hope, still hovering round Thy word,
Would light on some sweet promise there,
Some sure support against despair.

—R. A. Lapsley

*Wash me throughly from mine iniquity, and cleanse me from my sin.*
—Ps. 51:2

## FORGIVE ME

Forgive me, Lord, for careless words
    When hungry souls are near;
Words that are not of Faith and Love,
    Heavy with care and fear;

Forgive me for the words withheld,
    For words that might have won
A soul from darkened paths and sin
    To follow Thy dear Son.

Words are such mighty things, dear Lord,
    May I so yielded be
That Christ, who spake as never man,
    May ever speak through me.

—AUTHOR UNKNOWN

## FAITH

*Lord, I believe; help thou mine unbelief.*

—Mark 9:24

## MY PRAYER

If the way be rough with thorns and stones,
    May faith provide a balm
To soothe my weary, bleeding feet
    And fill my soul with calm.

—LUCY CARRUTH

## INCREASE OUR FAITH

Increase our faith, beloved Lord!
    For Thou alone canst give
The faith that takes Thee at Thy word,
    The faith by which we live.

*And the apostles said unto the Lord, Increase our faith.*—Luke 17:5

Increase our faith!  So weak are we,
   That we both may and must
Commit our very faith to Thee,
   Entrust to Thee our trust.

Increase our faith, that we may claim
   Each starry promise sure,
And always triumph in Thy name,
   And to the end endure.

Increase our faith, O Lord, we pray,
   That we may not depart
From Thy commands, but all obey
   With free and loyal heart.

Increase our faith, that never dim
   Or trembling it may be,
Crowned with the "perfect peace" of him
   "Whose mind is stayed on Thee."
               —FRANCES RIDLEY HAVERGAL


## LORD, GIVE ME FAITH

Lord, give me faith,
Enlightening faith,
   That I may see
      The things unseen
   With vision clear
      And crystalline.

Lord, give me faith,
Far-seeing faith,
   That I may tell
      My soul at night
   That in the sky
      The stars are bright.

*Be not faithless, but believing.*         —John 20:27

Lord, give me faith,
Assuring faith,
   That when I pass
     Deep glades of fear
   I'll realize
     That Thou art near.

Lord, give me faith,
Outreaching faith,
   That I, when tried,
     May flee to Thee,
   And find Thy strength
     My victory.

Lord, give me faith,
Revealing faith,
   That when I go
     Through cloud and storm
   I'll hear Thy voice
     And see Thy form.
         —DWIGHT EDWARDS MARVIN

## A PRAYER

Give me the faith that asks not "Why?"
I shall know God's plan by and by.

Give me the faith that looks at pain
And says all will be right again.

Give me the faith to bow my head
Trustfully waiting to be led.

*The just shall live by his faith.*         —Hab. 2:4

Give me the faith to face my life
With all its pain and wrong and strife,

And then with the day's setting sun
I'll close my eyes when life is done.

My soul will go without a care
Knowing that God is waiting there.

—AUTHOR UNKNOWN

## A PRAYER

Lord, give us more of faith,
   For, in our mortal sight,
Life and our little death
   Shut out the hills of light.

—NANCY BYRD TURNER

## FAITH

If I could feel my hand, dear Lord, in Thine
   And surely know
That I was walking in the light divine
   Through weal or woe;

If I could hear Thy voice in accents sweet
   But plainly say,
To guide my trembling, groping, wandering feet,
   "This is the way,"

I would so gladly walk therein, but now
   I cannot see.
Oh, give me, Lord, the faith to humbly bow
   And trust in Thee!

*And he said unto them, Why are ye so fearful? how is it that ye have
no faith?* —Mark 4:40

160

There is no *faith* in seeing.  Were we led
    Like children here,
And lifted over rock and river-bed,
    No care, no fear,

We should be useless in the busy throng,
    Life's work undone;
Lord, make us brave and earnest, true and strong,
    Till heaven is won.
               —SARAH K. BOLTON

## DOUBT

O distant Christ, the crowded, darkening years
    Drift slow between Thy gracious face and me;
    My hungry heart leans back to look for Thee,
But finds the way set thick with doubts and fears.

My groping hands would touch Thy garment's hem,
    Would find some token Thou art walking near;
    Instead, they clasp but empty darkness drear,
And no diviner hands reach out to them.

Sometimes my listening soul, with bated breath,
    Stands still to catch a footfall by my side,
    Lest, haply, my earth-blinded eyes but hide
Thy stately figure, leading Life and Death;

My straining eyes, O Christ, but long to mark
    A shadow of Thy presence, dim and sweet,
    Or far-off light to guide my wandering feet,
Or hope for hands prayer-beating 'gainst the dark.

*And Jesus, answering, saith unto them, Have faith in God.*
               —Mark 11:22

O Thou! unseen by me, that like a child
    Tries in the night to find its mother's heart,
    And weeping wanders only more apart,
Not knowing in the darkness that she smiled—

Thou, all unseen, dost hear my tired cry.
    As I, in darkness of a half-belief,
    Grope for Thy heart, in love and doubt and grief:
O Lord! speak soon to me—"Lo, here am I!"
                                    —MARGARET DELAND

# COURAGE

*Be strong and of a good courage; be not afraid, neither be thou dismayed: for the Lord thy God is with thee whithersoever thou goest.*
                                    —Josh. 1:9

## A PRAYER FOR COURAGE

God make me brave for life,
Oh, braver than this!
Let me straighten after pain.
As a tree straightens after the rain,
Shining and lovely again.

God make me brave for life,
Much braver than this!
As the blown grass lifts let me rise
From sorrow with quiet eyes,
Knowing Thy way is wise.

*Fear thou not; for I am with thee: be not dismayed; for I am thy God.*
                                    —Isa. 41:10

162

God make me brave—Life brings
Such blinding things.
Help me to keep my sight,
Help me to see aright
That out of the dark—comes light.
—GRACE NOLL CROWELL

## PRAYER FOR COURAGE

Why should I long for what I know
   Can never be revealed to me?
I only pray that I may grow
   As sure and bravely as a tree.

I do not ask why tireless grief
   Remains, or why all beauty flies;
I only crave the blind relief
   Of branches groping toward the skies.

Let me bring every seed to fruit,
   Sharing, whatever comes to pass,
The strong persistence of the root,
   The patient courage of the grass.

Heartened by every source of mirth,
   I shall not mind the wounds and scars,
Feeling the solid strength of earth,
   The bright conviction of the stars.
—LOUIS UNTERMEYER

## A PRAYER FOR COURAGE

Give me courage, Lord, to sail
   My boat out from the shore.
I'd rather know the ocean's gale
   And hear the tempest's roar

*Be of good courage, and he shall strengthen your heart, all ye that
hope in the Lord.*     —Ps. 31:24

Than anchor safely in some bay
   Because fear conquered me.
Let craft less daring inland stay—
   Be mine the pathless sea.
What though my boat at last go down,
I know my courage shall not drown.

Oh grant me aspiration, Lord,
   To seek the mountain's height;
The lowlands easy joy afford,
   But there 'tis soonest night.
My eyes shall watch the sun-lit peak
   As over rock and stone
I fall with ebbing strength, yet seek
   The upward ways alone.
Though not far from the base I stop
My soul shall climb on to the top.

Give me a valiant spirit, Lord,
   That bows not to defeat;
Though mine be but a broken sword
   Face-forward I would meet
The onrush on my armored foes,
   Nor beg on bended knee
That they withhold the fatal blows
   Which they intend for me.
The victory's mine if my last breath
Dare bid defiance still to death.

                —JOSEPH MORRIS

## A WOMAN'S PRAYER

O Lord, who knowest every need of mine,
Help me to bear each cross and not repine;

*They helped every one his neighbour; and every one said to his
brother, Be of good courage.*        —Isa. 41:6

Grant me fresh courage every day,
Help me to do my work alway
    Without complaint!

O Lord, Thou knowest well how dark the way,
Guide Thou my footsteps, lest they stray;
Give me fresh faith for every hour,
Lest I should ever doubt Thy power
    And make complaint!

Give me a heart, O Lord, strong to endure,
Help me to keep it simple, pure,
Make me unselfish, helpful, true
In every act, whate'er I do,
    And keep content!

Help me to do my woman's share,
Make me courageous, strong to bear
Sunshine or shadow in my life!
Sustain me in the daily strife
    To keep content!

—AUTHOR UNKNOWN

## SUSTAINING POWER

*Trust ye in the Lord for ever: for in the Lord Jehovah is everlasting strength.*

—Isa. 26:4

### THY STRENGTH AND MY DAY

Give me Thy strength for my day, Lord,
    That wheresoe'er I go,
There shall no danger daunt me
    And I shall fear no foe;

*As thy days, so shall thy strength be.*      —Deut. 33:25

So shall no task o'ercome me,
　　So shall no trial fret,
So shall I walk unwearied
　　The path where my feet are set;
So shall I find no burden
　　Greater than I can bear,
So shall I have a courage
　　Equal to all my care;
So shall no grief o'erwhelm me,
　　So shall no wave o'erflow:
Give me Thy strength for my day, Lord,
　　Cover my weakness so.
　　　　　　　　　　—ANNIE JOHNSON FLINT

## IN THE HOUR OF TRIAL

In the hour of trial,
　　Jesus, plead for me;
Lest by base denial,
　　I depart from Thee.
When Thou see'st me waver,
　　With a look recall,
Nor for fear or favor
　　Suffer me to fall.
　　　　　　　　　　—JAMES MONTGOMERY

## STRENGTH IN WEAKNESS

Lord, when my strength is weakness hitherto unknown,
　　When thought and deed are overborne with fear;
　　Lord, in Thy loving mercy be Thou near
When footsteps falter and I cannot walk alone.

"My child, I know thy need, and I am ever near
　　Thy weakness I provided for the hour,

*When I am weak, then am I strong.*　　　　—II Cor. 12:10

When perfected in weakness, then My power
Would steady faltering steps and banish all thy fear."

Lord, let me welcome weakness since it comes from Thee;
  I would not know the strength that comes of pride,
  Be Thou my strength though weakness still abide,
Since thus by grace Thy strength is perfected in me.
                                    —PHILIP E. HOWARD

## FOR DIVINE STRENGTH

Father, in thy mysterious presence kneeling,
  Fain would our souls feel all thy kindling love;
For we are weak and need some deep revealing
  Of trust, and strength, and calmness from above.

Lord, we have wandered far through doubt and sorrow,
  And thou hast made each step an onward one;
And we will ever trust each unknown morrow—
  Thou wilt sustain us till its work is done.

Now, Father, now, in thy dear presence kneeling,
  Our spirits yearn to feel thy kindling love;
Now make us strong, we need thy deep revealing,
  Of trust, and strength, and calmness from above.
                                    —SAMUEL JOHNSON

## AS WE PRAY

Only, O Lord, in Thy dear love
Fit us for perfect rest above;
And help us this and every day,
To live more nearly as we pray.
                                    —JOHN KEBLE

*Now therefore perform the doing of it; that as there was a readiness
to will, so there may be a performance.*          —II Cor. 8:11

## A PRAYER

We know the paths wherein our feet should press,
Across our hearts are written Thy decrees,
Yet now, O Lord, be merciful to bless
    With more than these.

Grant us the will to fashion as we feel,
Grant us the strength to labor as we know,
Grant us the purpose, ribbed and edged with steel,
    To strike the blow.

Knowledge we ask not—knowledge Thou hast lent,
But, Lord, the will—there lies our bitter need,
Give us to build above the deep intent
    The deed, the deed.

—JOHN DRINKWATER

## A PRAYER

Oh, not for more or longer days, dear Lord,
    My prayer shall be—
But rather teach me how to use the days
    Now given me.

I ask not more of pleasure or of joy
    For this brief while—
But rather let me for the joys I have
    Be glad and smile.

I ask not ownership of vast estates
    Nor piles of gold—
But make me generous with the little store
    My hands now hold.

*Let your conversation be without covetousness; and be content with such things as ye have.* —Heb. 13:5

Nor shall I ask that life should give to me
    Another friend—
Just keep me true to those I have, dear Lord,
    Until the end.

—B. Y. WILLIAMS

## A PRAYER

Not more of light I ask, O God,
    But eyes to see what is;
Not sweeter songs, but power to hear
    The present melodies.

Not greater strength, but how to use
    The power that I possess;
Not more of love, but skill to turn
    A frown to a caress.

Not more of joy, but power to feel
    Its kindling presence near,
To give to others all I have
    Of courage and of cheer.

Give me all fears to dominate,
    All holy joys to know;
To be the friend I wish to be,
    To speak the truth I know.

—FLORENCE HOLBROOK

*Well done, thou good and faithful servant: thou hast been faithful over a few things, I will make thee ruler over many things.*

—Matt. 25:21

## THY PEACE, O GOD

We bless Thee for Thy peace, O God,
　　Deep as th' unfathomed sea,
Which falls like sunshine on the road
　　Of those who trust in Thee.

We ask not, Father, for repose
　　Which comes from outward rest,
If we may have through all life's woes,
　　Thy peace within our breast.

That peace which suffers and is strong,
　　Trusts where it cannot see,
Deems not the trial way too long,
　　But leaves the end with Thee.

That peace which flows serene and deep,
　　A river in the soul,
Whose banks a living verdure keep,
　　God's sunshine o'er the whole.

O Father, give our hearts this peace,
　　Whate'er may outward be,
Till all life's discipline shall cease,
　　And we go home to Thee.
　　　　　　　　　—Author Unknown


## MY TIMES ARE IN THY HAND

Father, I know that all my life
　　Is portioned out for me,
And the changes that are sure to come
　　I do not fear to see;

*My times are in thy hand: deliver me from the hand of mine enemies,
and from them that persecute me.*　　　—Ps. 31:15

But I ask Thee for a patient mind,
    Intent on pleasing Thee.

I ask Thee for a thoughtful love,
    Through constant watching wise,
To meet the glad with joyful smiles,
    And wipe the weeping eyes;
And a heart at leisure from itself,
    To soothe and sympathize.

I would not have the restless will
    That hurries to and fro,
Seeking for some great thing to do,
    Or secret thing to know;
I would be dealt with as a child,
    And guided where I go.

So I ask for the daily strength,
    To none that ask denied,
And a mind to blend with outward life
    While keeping at Thy side.
Content to fill a little space,
    If Thou be glorified.

And if some things I do not ask,
    In my cup of blessing be,
I would have my spirit filled the more
    With grateful love to Thee;
And careful, than to serve Thee much,
    To please Thee perfectly.
                    —ANNA LAETITIA WARING

*For thou art my rock and my fortress: therefore, for thy name's sake, lead me and guide me.*                    —Ps. 31:3

## GUIDE ME

Being perplexed, I say,
   "Lord, make it right!
Night is as day to thee,
   Darkness is light.
I am afraid to touch
Things that involve so much;
My trembling hand may shake—
My skilless hand may break;
Thine can make no mistake."

Being in doubt, I say,
   "Lord, make it plain!
Which is the true, safe way?
   Which would be vain?
I am not wise to know,
Not sure of foot to go;
My blind eyes cannot see
What is so clear to thee;
Lord, make it clear to me."

—AUTHOR UNKNOWN

## MAKE THY WAY MINE

Father, hold thou my hands;
   The way is steep;
I cannot see the path my feet must keep,
I cannot tell, so dark the tangled way,
   Where next to step.  Oh stay;
Come close; take both my hands in thine;
   Make thy way mine!

*The steps of a good man are ordered by the Lord.*   —Ps. 37:23

Lead me. I may not stay;
I must move on; but oh, the way!
I must be brave and go,
Step forward in the dark, nor know
If I shall reach the goal at all—
If I shall fall.
Take thou my hand.
Take it! Thou knowest best
How I should go, and all the rest
I cannot, cannot see:
Lead me: I hold my hands to thee;
I own no will but thine;
Make thy way mine!

—GEORGE KLINGLE

## GUIDANCE

My little daughter leans upon my arms,
  Close to my heart—leans hard upon my strength,
I guide her unskilled hand. Tenderness warms
  My being for her weakness, till at length—
The task achieved—I say, "Well done, my child,"
    And she runs off to play,
    Her lesson learned,
    And commendation earned.


So, Father, leans my weakness on Thy love,
  My unskilled hand take Thou, dear God, in Thine.
Forgive the feeble effort, the wrong move,
  Help me to shape my life by Thine;

*Thus saith the Lord; Behold, I set before you the way of life.*
                              —Jer. 21:8

173

Steady my hand for the appointed task,
Till comes the longed-for day
When Thou at last canst say,
"Well done, my child."

—Harriet B. Williams

# COMFORT

*As one whom his mother comforteth, so will I comfort you.*
—Isa. 66:13

## PRAYER

Dear Refuge of my weary soul,
On Thee, when sorrows rise,
On Thee, when waves of trouble roll,
My fainting hope relies.

To Thee I tell each rising grief,
For Thou alone canst heal;
Thy word can bring a sweet relief,
For every pain I feel.

—Anne Steele

## PRAYER IN SORROW

Father, to Thee we look in all our sorrow,
Thou art the fountain whence our healing flows;
Dark though the night, joy cometh with the morrow;
Safely they rest who in Thy love repose.

When fond hopes fail and skies are dark before us,
When the vain cares that vex our life increase—
Comes with its calm the thought that Thou art o'er us,
And we grow quiet, folded in Thy peace.

*For I will turn their mourning into joy, and will comfort them, and make them rejoice from their sorrow.* —Jer. 31:13

174

Naught shall affright us on thy goodness leaning,
   Low in the heart Faith singeth still her song;
Chastened by pain, we learn life's deepest meaning,
   And in our weakness Thou dost make us strong.

Patient, O heart, though heavy be thy sorrows!
   Be not cast down, disquieted in vain;
Yet shalt thou praise Him when these darkened furrows,
   Where now He plougheth, wave with golden grain.

              —FREDERICK L. HOSMER

## AS I GROW OLD

God keep my heart attuned to laughter
     When youth is done;
When all the days are gray days, coming after
     The warmth, the sun.
Ah! keep me then from bitterness, from grieving,
     When life seems cold;
God keep me always loving and believing
     As I grow old.

             —AUTHOR UNKNOWN

## BE MERCIFUL

Once ran my prayer as runs the brook
   Over pebbles and through sunny meads;
No pain my inmost spirit shook,
   Words broke in shallows of small needs.

But now the shadows on me lie,
   Deep-cut the channel of the years;
And prayer is but a sobbing cry
   Through whitened lips and falling tears.

*Because thou hast been my help, therefore in the shadow of thy wings
will I rejoice.*          —Ps. 63:7

Not glibly, but with broken speech,
O God, my God, I pray to thee;
Enough if now I may beseech,
Be merciful, O God, to me!
—JOHN T. MCFARLAND

## AT LAST

When on my day of life the night is falling,
And, in the winds from unsunned spaces blown,
I hear far voices out of darkness calling
My feet to paths unknown,

Thou who hast made my home of life so pleasant,
Leave not its tenant when its walls decay;
O Love Divine, O Helper ever present,
Be Thou my strength and stay!

Be near me when all else is from me drifting:
Earth, sky, home's pictures, days of shade and shine,
And kindly faces to my own uplifting
The love which answers mine.

I have but Thee, my Father! let Thy spirit
Be with me then to comfort and uphold;
No gate of pearl, no branch of palm I merit,
Nor street of shining gold.

Suffice it if—my good and ill unreckoned,
And both forgiven through Thy abounding grace—
I find myself by hands familiar beckoned
Unto my fitting place.
—JOHN GREENLEAF WHITTIER

*And if I go and prepare a place for you, I will come again, and receive
you unto myself; that where I am, there ye may be also.*—John 14:3

## DEATH

To fold my hands a little while in sleep
A brief night through, and wait with quiet breath
The coming of the morning, and to keep
Quite calm and still, is that what we call death?
Is it a thing to fear, O Lord of life,
O Lord of death, O Lord of the unknown:
To heed no more the clamor and the strife,
To rest a bit, uncomraded, alone,
Save with Thee, Lord, who hast the power to keep
Thine own.

And with Thee, Lord, why should I fear to wait
A little while until my eyes shall see,
Or whether I shall wake me soon or late,
So long as Thy cupped hand is holding me?
Grant, Father, when the night comes, I shall rise
With willing feet, and fold my work away;
Then, lying down to sleep, close fearless eyes,
Regretful not of further work or play,
But in the sleep Thou givest Thy beloved
Await the day.

—GRACE NOLL CROWELL

## THE OTHER ROOM

Lord, I doubt no more Thy mercy,
Think no more of death as doom,
But the stepping o'er the threshold
To the bigger, brighter room.

—AUTHOR UNKNOWN

*For we know, that if our earthly house of this tabernacle were dissolved, we have a building of God, an house not made with hands, eternal in the heavens.* —II Cor. 5:1

## NEARING THE FORD

Kindle, O Lord, along the way
Bright guiding torches, lest I stray;
   For I am near the ford.
Take Thou my hand, clear Thou my sight
Amid these brooding clouds of night:
   Kindle the torches, Lord.

The mists are falling o'er my eyes
And darkness robes the dripping skies
   As I draw near the ford.
Strange voices whisper in my ear;
Strange thoughts surcharge my mind with fear:
   Kindle the torches, Lord.

The waters roar, I cannot see
And tremble with anxiety,
   Now I am near the ford.
Light Thou the lonely path I tread;
Take from my mind all doubt and dread:
   Kindle the torches, Lord.

Behold, One cometh on apace,
A radiance gleaming from His face,
   He calls, "Fear not the ford."
His garments are as white as snow,
And on my path there falls a glow
   Brighter than torches, Lord.

I cannot suffer harm or loss
When I the rushing waters cross;
   For He is at the ford.

*When thou passest through the waters, I will be with thee.*
                   —Isa. 43:2

Soon I shall go through portals bright
To walk with Him in realms of light
   And need no torches, Lord.
                    —Dwight Edwards Marvin

## LIGHT AT EVENING TIME

Holy Father, cheer our way
With thy love's perpetual ray;
Grant us every closing day
   Light at evening time.

Holy Saviour, calm our fears
When earth's brightness disappears;
Grant us in our later years
   Light at evening time.

Holy Spirit, be thou nigh
When in mortal pains we lie;
Grant us, as we come to die.
   Light at evening time.

Holy, blessèd Trinity,
Darkness is not dark to thee;
Those thou keepest always see
   Light at evening time.
                    —R. H. Robinson

# SUPPLEMENT

## Poems About Prayer

THE CALL TO PRAYER

THE MEANING OF PRAYER

THE METHOD OF PRAYER

THE FELLOWSHIP OF PRAYER

THE RESULTS OF PRAYER

# Poems About Prayer

## THE CALL TO PRAYER

*Call unto me, and I will answer thee, and shew thee great and mighty things, which thou knowest not.*

—Jer. 33:3

Speak to Him thou for He hears, and Spirit with Spirit can
    meet—
Closer is He than breathing, and nearer than hands and feet.
—ALFRED TENNYSON


## PRAY!

"Men ought always to pray."—Luke 18:1

Pray in the early morning
  For grace throughout the day;
We know not what temptations
  And trials may cross our way.

Pray in the gladsome noontide,
  When the day is at its best;
Pray when the night o'ertakes thee
  To Him who giveth rest.

*Ask, and it shall be given you.*
    —Matt. 7:7

Pray in the silent midnight,
    If wakeful hours be thine;
Pray for a heart submissive,
    That never will repine.

Pray in the hour of sorrow,
    Pray in the hour of grief;
In coming to the Father,
    Thy soul shall find relief.

Pray when the sun shines brightest,
    Thy path with roses strewn;
Pray that thy heart be ever
    With the Saviour's kept in tune.

Pray when the dark day cometh,
    And clouds hang overhead;
In the secret of His presence
    Thy soul hath naught to dread.

Pray for the Father's guidance
    In all thy work and ways,
So shall thy days be fruitful,
    Thy life be full of praise.

Living in touch with Jesus,
    Keeping our own hearts right,
Others will be attracted
    From darkness into light.

—IRENE ARNOLD


## SEEK THE LORD IN PRAYER

Wouldst thou know the way to lighten
    Every load of grief and care!
Seek the presence of the Saviour,
    Carry all to Him in prayer.

*Let us therefore come boldly unto the throne of grace.*—Heb. 4:16

184

Wouldst thou find the joy of being
    Used of Jesus everywhere?
Closely walk beside the Master
    Often seek His face in prayer.

Wouldst thou have a power for service,
    In life's conquest have a share?
Lean upon the Arm Almighty,
    Spend much time with God in prayer.

Wouldst thou have divine enrichment—
    Grace for all you have to bear?
God will bless with richest measure,
    All who go to Him in prayer.
                —AUTHOR UNKNOWN

## THE SENTINEL

The morning is the gate of day,
    But ere you enter there
See that you set to guard it well,
    The sentinel of prayer.

So shall God's grace your steps attend,
    But nothing else pass through
Save what can give the countersign;
    The Father's will for you.

When you have reached the end of day
    Where night and sleep await,
Set there the sentinel again
    To bar the evening's gate.

*Call ye upon him while he is near.*        —Isa. 55:6

So shall no fear disturb your rest,
No danger and no care.
For only peace and pardon pass
The watchful guard of prayer.

—ANNIE JOHNSON FLINT

## OUR BURDEN BEARER

The little sharp vexations
And the briars that cut the feet,
Why not take all to the Helper
Who has never failed us yet?
Tell him about the heartache,
And tell him the longings too,
Tell him the baffled purpose
When we scarce know what to do.
Then, leaving all our weakness
With the One divinely strong,
Forget that we bore the burden
And carry away the song.

—PHILLIPS BROOKS

## STRIVE, WAIT AND PRAY

Pray: though the gift you ask for
May never comfort your fears,
May never repay your pleading,
Yet pray, and with hopeful tears;
An answer, not that you long for,
But diviner, will come one day;
Your eyes are too dim to see it,
Yet strive, and wait, and pray.

—ADELAIDE ANNE PROCTER

*Then shall ye call upon me, . . . . and I will hearken unto you.*
—Jer. 29:12

## PRAY!

Pray! for earth has many a need.
Pray! for prayer is vital deed.
Pray! for God in heaven hears.
Pray! prayer will move the spheres.
Pray! for praying leads to peace.
Pray! for praying gives release.
Pray! for prayer is never lost.
Pray! for prayer well pays its cost.
Pray! for prayer is always power.
Pray! for every prayer's a flower.
Pray! for prayer the Saviour finds.
Pray! for prayer creation binds.
Pray! for every prayer is gold.
Pray! for prayer is joy untold.
Pray! for praying frees from care.
Pray! for Jesus joins your prayer.

—Amos R. Wells

## PRAYER

But since He heareth prayer at any time,
For anything, in any place, or clime,
Men lightly value Heaven's choicest gift,
And all too seldom do their souls uplift
In earnest pleading at the Throne of Grace.
Oh, let us then more often seek His face,
With grateful hearts, remembering while there
To thank our Father that He heareth prayer.

—Author Unknown

*Seek the Lord and his strength, seek his face continually.*
—I Chron. 16:11

## WITH GOD

Begin the day with God:
   Kneel down to him in prayer;
Lift up thy heart to his abode
   And seek his love to share.

Open the Book of God,
   And read a portion there;
That it may hallow all thy thoughts
   And sweeten all thy care.

Go through the day with God,
   Whate'er thy work may be;
Where'er thou art—at home, abroad,
   He still is near to thee.

Conclude the day with God:
   Thy sins to him confess;
Trust in the Lord's atoning blood,
   And plead his righteousness.

Lie down at night with God,
   Who gives his servants sleep.
And when thou tread'st the vale of death
   He will thee guard and keep.
            —AUTHOR UNKNOWN

## TELL IT TO GOD

When you waken in the morning,
   Ere you tread the untried way
Of the lot that lies before you
   Through the coming busy day;

*If thou seek him, he will be found of thee.*    —I Chron. 28:9

Whether sunbeams promise brightness,
  Whether dim forebodings fall,
Be the dawning glad or gloomy,
  Go to God—and tell Him all.


In the calm of sweet communion
  Let your daily work be done;
In the peace of soul-outpouring,
  Care be banished, patience won;
And if earth with its enchantments
  Seeks your spirit to enthrall,
Ere you listen—ere you answer—
  Go to God—and tell Him all.


Then as hour by hour glides by you,
  You will His blessed guidance know,
Your own burdens being lightened,
  You can bear another's woe;
You can help the weak ones onward,
  You can raise up those who fall—
But remember, while you're serving,
  Go to God—and tell Him all.


And if weariness creep o'er you
  As the day wears to its close,
Or if sudden fierce temptation
  Brings you face to face with foes;
In your weakness, in your peril,
  Raise to Heaven a trustful call,
Strength He gives for every crisis—
  Go to God—and tell Him all.

—DOROTHY DIX PORGES

*Seek ye me, and ye shall live.*                    —Amos 5:4

## PRAYER

When in the morning hour you rise,
Lift up to God thy grateful eyes,
And breathe to Him, whilst waiting there,
A word of humble praise and prayer.
For thou, poor mortal, needs must come—
As day by day you journey home—
Close to the Father-heart above,
If thou wouldst know a Father's love.

—W. T. PEARMAN

# THE MEANING OF PRAYER

*I cried to thee, O Lord; and unto the Lord I made supplication.*
—Ps. 30:8

## PRAYER

Prayer is work, dost thou believe it?
Prayer is power, wilt thou receive it?
Prayer the path the Saviour trod,
Prayer the touch that links with God.
Make thy life a daily prayer,
He will answer—here and there.

—AUTHOR UNKNOWN

## WHAT IS PRAYER?

Prayer is the soul's sincere desire,
Uttered or unexpressed—
The motion of a hidden fire,
That kindles in the breast.

*Thou heardest the voice of my supplications, when I cried unto thee.*
—Ps. 31:22

Prayer is the burthen of a sigh,
   The falling of a tear—
The upward glancing of an eye,
   When none but God is near.

Prayer is the simplest form of speech
   That infant lips can try—
Prayer the sublimest strains that reach
   The majesty on high.

Prayer is the contrite sinner's voice
   Returning from his ways,
While angels in their songs rejoice,
   And cry, "Behold! He prays!"

Prayer is the Christian's vital breath—
   The Christian's native air—
His watchword at the gates of death—
   He enters heaven with prayer.

The saints in prayer appear as one
   In words and deed and mind,
Where with the Father and the Son
   Sweet fellowship they find.

Nor prayer is made by man alone—
   The Holy Spirit pleads—
And Jesus, on the eternal throne,
   For sinners intercedes.

O Thou by whom we come to God—
   The Life, the Truth, the Way!
The path of prayer Thyself hast trod;
   Lord, teach us how to pray.

               —JAMES MONTGOMERY

*Evening, and morning, and at noon, will I pray, and cry aloud; and
he shall hear my voice.*           —Ps. 55:17

## THE STAIRWAY TO THE STARS

There's a stairway leading upward—
  Which the weariest may climb
Far above the highest mountain
  To an altitude sublime,
Where a Comforter awaits us,
  For the Father's home is there;
And the way to mount that stairway
  Is the simple way of prayer!

There's a stairway leading upward—
  Though the distance may be far,
Though the lowest step's a valley,
  And the highest step a star;
'Tis the measure of an instant,
  Lowly vale to starry height—
Just a little prayer will lift us
  From the darkness to the light.

—WILLIAM LUDLUM

## THE UNSEEN BRIDGE

There is a bridge, whereof the span
Is rooted in the heart of man,
And reaches, without pile or rod,
Unto the Great White Throne of God.

Its traffic is in human sighs
Fervently wafted to the skies;
'Tis the one pathway from Despair;
And it is called the Bridge of Prayer.

—GILBERT THOMAS

*Be still, and know that I am God.*                    —Ps. 46:10

## WHAT IS PRAYER?

What is prayer but listening in—
   Attuning
Mind and heart to hear
A still small voice beyond life's sin,
   Assured that God is ever near?

What is prayer but lifting all
   Our longings,
Fraught with tears and praise,
To Him who knows the sparrow's fall
   And answers in uncounted ways?
            —MARIE BARTON

## THE MEANING OF PRAYER

A breath of prayer in the morning
   Means a day of blessing sure—
A breath of prayer in the evening
   Means a night of rest secure.

A breath of prayer in our weakness
   Means the clasp of a mighty Hand—
A breath of prayer when we're lonely
   Means Someone to understand.

A breath of prayer in rejoicing
   Gives joy and added delight.
For they that remember God's goodness
   Go singing far into the night.

There's never a year nor a season
   That prayer may not bless every hour

*My prayer is unto thee, O Lord.*        —Ps. 69:13

And never a soul need be helpless
When linked with God's infinite power.
—AUTHOR UNKNOWN

## THE PEACE OF PRAYER

I cast my care on Him
And sing again;
For God's love makes me smile
Through heavy pain.
And oh, when His dear face
The dark clouds dim,
And leave me all alone
Weeping for Him,
Mourning for friends who left
My heart in dust,
Lo, grief is turned to joy
Because I trust!
Prayer is His children's life,
Their rest from care;
How poor the heart which spurns
The peace of prayer!
—HONAMI NAGATA (a leper)
Trans. by LOIS J. ERICKSON

# THE METHOD OF PRAYER

*One of his disciples said unto him, Lord, teach us to pray.*
—Luke 11:1

## THE SECRET

I met God in the morning
When my day was at its best,
And his presence came like sunrise,
Like a glory in my breast.

*Blessed are all they that put their trust in him.*        —Ps. 2:12

All day long the Presence lingered,
  All day long he stayed with me,
And we sailed in perfect calmness
  O'er a very troubled sea.

Other ships were blown and battered,
  Other ships were sore distressed,
But the winds that seemed to drive them
  Brought to us a peace and rest.

Then I thought of other mornings,
  With a keen remorse of mind,
When I too had loosed the moorings,
  With the Presence left behind.

So I think I know the secret,
  Learned from many a troubled way:
You must seek him in the morning
  If you want him through the day!
                    —RALPH S. CUSHMAN

## A MOMENT IN THE MORNING

A moment in the morning, ere the cares of day begin,
Ere the heart's wide door is open for the world to enter in;
Ah, then alone with Jesus, in the silence of the morn,
In heavenly, sweet communion let your duty day be born.
In the quietude that blesses with a prelude of repose,
Let your soul be soothed and softened, as the dew revives the rose.

A moment in the morning, take your Bible in your hand,
And catch a glimpse of glory from the peaceful promised land;
It will linger still before you when you seek the busy mart,
And, like flowers of hope, will blossom into beauty in your heart;

*And in the morning, rising up a great while before day, he went out,
and departed into a solitary place, and there prayed.*—Mark 1:35

The precious words, like jewels, will glisten all the day,
With a rare, effulgent glory that will brighten all the way.

A moment in the morning—a moment, if no more—
Is better than an hour when the trying day is o'er.
'Tis the gentle dew from heaven, the manna for the day;
If you fail to gather early—alas! it melts away.
So, in the blush of morning take the offered hand of love,
And walk in heaven's pathway and the peacefulness thereof.
—ARTHUR LEWIS TUBBS

## PRAYER TIME

The while she darns her children's socks,
　　She prays for little stumbling feet;
Each folded pair within its box
　　Fits faith's bright sandals, sure and fleet.

While washing out, with mother pains,
　　Small dusty suits and frocks and slips,
She prays that God may cleanse the stains
　　From little hearts and hands and lips.

And when she breaks the fragrant bread,
　　Or pours each portion in its cup,
For grace to keep their spirits fed,
　　Her mother-heart is lifted up.

O busy ones, whose souls grow faint,
　　Whose tasks seem longer than the day,
It doesn't take a cloistered saint
　　To find a little time to pray!
—RUBY WEYBURN TOBIAS

*If any man hear my voice, and open the door, I will come in to him,
and will sup with him, and he with me.*　　　—Rev. 3:20

## TOO BUSY?

"I'm busy!
   No, I cannot stay,
A thousand things
   Call me away;
To-morrow
   I will stop to pray."
*And so I lost me*
   *One great day!*

"I'm busy!
   Yes, so I must wait,
A thousand things
   Without my gate
Warn that to-morrow
   Is too late
To pray."
*And so I saved me*
   *One great day!*

—RALPH S. CUSHMAN

## PRAYERLESSNESS

"No time to pray!"
Oh! who so fraught with earthly care
As not to give to humble prayer
   Some part of day?

"No time to pray!"
'Mid each day's dangers what retreat
More needful than the mercy seat?
   Who need to pray?

*And he spake a parable unto them to this end, that men ought always*
*to pray, and not to faint.*                    —Luke 18:1

"No time to pray!"
Must care or business' urgent call
So press it as to take it all,
    Each passing day?

    What thought more dread
Than that our God His face should hide,
And say through all life's swelling tide,
    "No time to hear!"
                                    —AUTHOR UNKNOWN

## SWEET HOUR OF PRAYER!

Sweet hour of prayer! sweet hour of prayer!
That calls me from a world of care,
And bids me at my Father's throne
Make all my wants and wishes known:
In seasons of distress and grief,
My soul has often found relief;
And oft escaped the tempter's snare,
By thy return, sweet hour of prayer!
                            —WILLIAM W. WALFORD

## THE PLACE OF PRAYER

The place of prayer is a humble place,
    And ere we enter there
We must leave outside our garb of pride
    And our load of worldly care.

The place of prayer is a quiet place,
    And at the outer gate
The voice of our will we must firmly still,
    And bid our wishes wait.

*But thou, when thou prayest, enter into thy closet, and when thou
hast shut thy door, pray to thy Father which is in secret.*
                                    —Matt. 6:6

The place of prayer is a holy place,
 And ere we step therein,
With unshod feet our God to meet,
 We must put away our sin.

But the place of prayer is high enough
 To bring heaven's glory nigh,
And our need speaks clear to our Father's ear,
 And is open to His eye.

And the place of prayer is wide enough
 For Christ to enter there;
And the humble heart need not depart
 Without that vision fair.

And the place of prayer is large enough
 To hold God's riches stored,
And faith is the key of the treasury
 That opens the secret hoard.

      —ANNIE JOHNSON FLINT

## THE SHUT DOOR

I need not leave the jostling world,
 Or wait till daily tasks are o'er,
To fold my palms in secret prayer
 Within the close-shut, closet door.

There is a viewless, cloistered room,
 As high as heaven, as fair as day,
Where though my feet may join the throng,
 My soul can enter in and pray.

*God is a Spirit: and they that worship him must worship him in spirit
and in truth.*       —John 4:24

And never through those crystal walls
   The clash of life can pierce its way,
Nor ever can a human ear
   Drink in the spirit-words I say.


One hearkening, even, cannot know
   When I have crossed the threshold o'er;
For He alone, who hears my prayer,
   Has heard the shutting of the door.

                    —AUTHOR UNKNOWN


## INTO A MOUNTAIN APART

### Matthew 14:23

The multitudes thronged
   Into the valley
In eagerness day after day,
But Jesus alone,
   As the sun sank to rest,
Drew apart in the mountain
   To pray.


In fellowship sweet
   With His Father,
Their mutual affection to share,
And sometimes His vigil
   Would last the night through,
For the daybreak would find Him
   In prayer.


*And when he had sent the multitudes away, he went up into a mountain apart to pray: and when the evening was come, he was there alone.*        —Matt. 14:23

His burdens were left
  In the mountain,
His strength, as the eagle's renewed,
The Master returned,
  With His courage newborn,
And His arduous labors
  Pursued.

Thus Jesus has taught
  His disciples,
The duty and privilege of prayer,
We, too, must ascend
  To the mountain apart,
In that sacred communion
  To share.

—ALICE E. SHERWOOD


# I LOVE TO STEAL AWHILE AWAY

I love to steal awhile away
  From every cumbering care,
And spend the hours of setting day
  In humble, grateful prayer.

I love in solitude to shed
  The penitential tear,
And all his promises to plead,
  Where none but God can hear.

I love to think on mercies past,
  And future good implore,
And all my cares and sorrows cast
  On him whom I adore.

—PHOEBE H. BROWN

*And he said unto them, Come ye yourselves apart into a desert place, and rest a while.*
                                        —Mark 6:31

# THE FAULT IS MINE

Sometimes God seems so far away,
  The mists between so dense,
My heart is filled with sudden dread,
  Foreboding, and suspense.
The very prayers I utter
  Come straightway back through space—
Too weak to make their faltering way
  Up to the throne of grace.

And then again, God seems so near,
  I cannot but believe;
His faintest whisper rings as clear
  As vesper chimes at eve.
"I never leave thee nor forsake,"
  His gentle whisper saith;
And what had caused my sudden dread
  Was just my lack of faith!
                    —Edith M. Lee

# PRAY WITH FAITH

Prayer is appointed to convey
  The blessings God designs to give:
Long as they live should Christians pray;
  They learn to pray when first they live.

'Tis prayer supports the soul that's weak;
  Though thought be broken, language lame,
Pray, if thou canst or canst not speak;
  But pray with faith in Jesus' name.

*If ye have faith, . . . . nothing shall be impossible unto you.*
                    —Matt. 17:20

Depend on him; thou canst not fail;
  Make all thy wants and wishes known;
Fear not; his merits must prevail:
  Ask but in faith, it shall be done.
                              —Joseph Hart

## SHALL I PRAY ON?

For years I've prayed, and yet I see no change.
The mountain stands exactly where it stood;
  The shadows that it casts are just as deep;
  The pathway to its summit e'en more steep.
        Shall I pray on?

Shall I pray on with ne'er a hopeful sign?
Not only does the mountain still remain
  But, while I watch to see it disappear,
  Becomes the more appalling year by year.
        Shall I pray on?

I will pray on.  Though distant it may seem,
The answer may be almost at my door,
  Or just around the corner on its way.
  But whether near or far, yea, I shall pray—
        I will pray on.
                              —Edith L. Mapes

## COME, MY SOUL, THY SUIT PREPARE

Come, my soul, thy suit prepare,
Jesus loves to answer prayer;
He himself has bid thee pray,
Therefore will not say thee nay.

*What things soever ye desire when ye pray, believe that ye receive
them, and ye shall have them.*                    —Mark 11:24

203

Thou art coming to a King;
Large petitions with thee bring;
For his grace and power are such,
None can ever ask too much.

JOHN NEWTON

## THE LARGER PRAYER

At first I prayed for Light:—
  Could I but see the way,
How gladly, swiftly would I walk
  To everlasting day!

And next I prayed for Strength:—
  That I might tread the road
With firm, unfaltering feet, and win
  The heaven's serene abode.

And then I asked for Faith:—
  Could I but trust my God,
I'd live enfolded in his peace,
  Though foes were all abroad.

But now I pray for Love;
  Deep love to God and man;
A living love that will not fail,
  However dark his plan;—

And Light and Strength and Faith
  Are opening everywhere!
God only waited for me till
  I prayed the larger prayer.

—EDNAH D. CHENEY

*Praying always with all prayer and supplication in the Spirit, and watching thereunto with all perseverance and supplication.*
—Eph. 6:18

## REVELATION

I knelt to pray when day was done,
And prayed, "O Lord, bless everyone;
Lift from each saddened heart the pain,
And let the sick be well again."
And then I woke another day
And carelessly went on my way.
The whole day long I did not try
To wipe a tear from any eye;
I did not try to share the load
Of any brother on my road;
I did not even go to see
The sick man just next door to me.
Yet once again when day was done
I prayed, "O Lord, bless everyone."
But as I prayed, into my ear
There came a voice that whispered clear:
"Pause, hypocrite, before you pray,
Whom have you tried to bless today?
God's sweetest blessings always go
By hands that serve Him here below."
And then I hid my face, and cried,
"Forgive me, God, for I have lied;
Let me but see another day
And I will live the way I pray."

—WHITNEY MONTGOMERY

## PRAYER AND DEEDS

No answer comes to those who pray,
    Then idly stand
And wait for stones to roll away

*God is love; and he that dwelleth in love dwelleth in God, and God in him.* —I John 4:16

205

At God's command.
He will not break the binding cords
    Upon us laid
If we depend on pleading words,
    And do not aid.
When hands are idle, words are vain
    To move the stone;
An abiding angel would disdain
    To work alone;
But he who prayeth and is strong
    In faith and deed,
And toileth earnestly, ere long
    He will succeed.

—AUTHOR UNKNOWN

## THANKSGIVING

It is fine to say we're thankful
    For all that we possess,
It is fine to put it plainly
    In words and not suppress
One item in the total score;
    But if our thanks be true—
We'll prove it, not so much in words
    As by the deeds we do.

The act speaks louder than the word,
    And though our words be good—
The little deeds in kindness done
    Are better understood;
Thanksgiving may be given voice
    In tones which loudly ring;

*Whatsoever ye would that men should do to you, do ye even so to them.*                                        —Matt. 7:12

But to show best true thankfulness—
  Thanksliving—is the thing.
                    —William Ludlum

## WHEN SAINT CHRYSOSTOM PRAYED

'Twas not enough to kneel in prayer,
  And pour his very soul away
  In fervid wrestlings, night and day,
For those who owned his shepherd care;
But faith and works went hand in hand,
  As test of each petition made,
And saints were helped throughout the land
  When Saint Chrysostom prayed.

Within the closet where he knelt,
  A box of Bethlehem's olive-wood—
  "For Christ," engraved upon it—stood;
And ever as he daily felt
The pressure of the Church's need,
  Therein the daily gift was laid;
For word had instant proof of deed
  When Saint Chrysostom prayed.

Beneath his folded hands he placed
  Whatever gold was his; and when
  He travailed for the souls of men,
So long by Pagan rites debased,
The more he agonized, the more
  The burden of his spirit weighed;
And piece by piece went all his store,
  When Saint Chrysostom prayed.

O golden-mouthed, let this thine alms
  Rouse us to shame, who daily bow

*Freely ye have received, freely give.*            —Matt. 10:8

Within our secret places now,
With outstretched yet with empty palms!
We supplicate indeed; but has
    Our faith brought answering works to aid?
Have words by deeds been proven, as
    When Saint Chrysostom prayed?
                              —Margaret J. Preston


# THE FELLOWSHIP OF PRAYER

*Where two or three are gathered together in my name, there am
I in the midst of them.*

—Matt. 18:20


## INTERCEDING

I dreamed the Saviour came to be
    My Guest awhile,
My home was hallowed by His word,
    His gracious smile.
At evening in the chamber there
    He went alone;
I listened breathlessly to hear
    An undertone
That thrilled my very soul because
    It held my name!
Oh, was it all an empty dream?
    Nay, just the same
As if within that little room
    I heard Him pray,
He brings my need before the Father
    Every day.

—Opal Leonore Gibbs

*He is able also to save them to the uttermost that come unto God by
him, seeing he ever liveth to make intercession for them.*

—Heb. 7:25

## OUR HIGH PRIEST

He is our great High Priest today;
   Within the riven veil He stands,
The sacrifice forever made,
   The shed blood still upon His hands;
Those wounded hands our pardon win,
   His mediation cannot fail,
Our Advocate pleads not in vain,
   Our Intercessor must prevail.
           —ANNIE JOHNSON FLINT

## INTERCESSION

That sacred, solemn night, the last on earth—
'Twas Christ's to share their daily round of life—
He prayed for them, His own, and prayed for me.

After the glad ascension day had come,
At God's right hand upon His throne, He sat
And prayed for them, His own, and prays for me.

His own for whom He prayed, for others prayed,
And these for others importuned, till link
By link a golden chain was forged—

A golden chain that binds my life to His.
I kneel to forge another golden link;
And, oh, my friend! my friend! I pray for you!
           —L. M. HOLLINGSWORTH

## PRAY FOR ME!

I beg of you calm souls—whose wondering pity
   Looks at paths you never trod;

*Neither pray I for these alone, but for them also which shall believe
on me through their word.*         —John 17:20

I beg of you who suffer—for all sorrow
  Must be very near to God—
And the need is even greater than you see—
    Pray for me!

I beg of you who stand before the Altar,
  Whose anointed hands upraise
All the Sin and all the Sorrow of the Ages,
  All the Love and all the Praise,
And the Glory which was always, and shall be—
    Pray for me!
                                —ADELAIDE ANNE PROCTER

## PRAY FOR ME

On faith's mysterious heights you stand,
And reach and grasp the Father's hand.
Oh, with that access bold and free,
Place a petition there for me!

I grope in fogs.  Your vision, clear
In faith's serener atmosphere,
Oh, use victoriously for me,
And paint the heaven I cannot see!

Too cold my tongue, too dull my ear,
Earth's nobler words to speak or hear.
Oh, while I learn the lower song,
Sing you for me in heaven's throng!

Still for myself I'll work and pray,
And toil along my blundering way;
But doubled all my strength will be
If you, O friend, will pray for me!
                                —AMOS R. WELLS

*I have prayed for thee, that thy faith fail not.*        —Luke 22:32

## PRAY ONE FOR ANOTHER

I cannot tell why there should come to me
    A thought of someone miles and miles away,
In swift insistence on the memory,
    Unless a need there be that I should pray.

Too hurried oft are we to spare the thought
    For days together, of some friends away;
Perhaps God does it for us, and we ought
    To read His signal as a call to pray.

Perhaps, just then, my friend has fiercer fight
    And more appalling weakness, and decay
Of courage, darkness, some lost sense of right—
    And so, in case he needs my prayer, I pray.

Friend, do the same for me.  If I intrude
    Unasked upon you, on some crowded day,
Give me a moment's prayer as interlude;
    Be very sure I need it, therefore pray.

And when thou prayest, friend, I ask of thee
    That thou wilt seek of God not mine own way,
Not what I want, but His best thought for me;
    Do thou through Jesus Christ implore, I pray.

              —MARIANNE FARNINGHAM

          Last stanza, JAMES M. GRAY

## THE PRAYER MEETING

We meet—one another, and friendship expands
As eye catches eye, and as hands welcome hands.

*In thy presence is fulness of joy; at thy right hand there are pleasures
for evermore.*           —Ps. 16:11

The touch of good fellowship thrills to the soul,
And each is inspired by the zeal of the whole.

We meet—the dear Saviour, unseen and unheard;
We leap to the vision, we feed on the word;
His presence, so loving, so wise, and so strong,
Is felt in each moment of prayer or of song.

We meet—our ideals; exulting we see
The grace that our living might blessedly be.
We burn with the joy of that promised delight
And spring to achieve it in heaven-born might!

So meeting, we practice the life of true men;
So parting, we part but to gather again;
Till soon—how the spirit awaits it and yearns!—
We shall meet in the meeting that never adjourns.
—AMOS R. WELLS

## AT PRAYER MEETING

There were only two or three of us
    Who came to the place of prayer;
Came in the teeth of a driving storm;
    But for that we did not care,
Since after our hymns of praise had risen,
    And our earnest prayers were said,
The Master Himself was present there
    And gave us the living bread.

We knew His look in our leader's face,
    So rapt and glad and free;

*For where two or three are gathered together in my name, there am
I in the midst of them.* —Matt. 18:20

We felt His touch when our heads we bowed,
   We heard His "Come to Me!"
Nobody saw Him lift the latch,
   And none unbarred the door;
But peace was His token to every heart,
   And how could we ask for more?

It was only a handful gathered in
   To the little place of prayer,
Outside was struggle and pain and sin,
   But the Lord Himself was there;
He came to redeem the pledge He gave
   Wherever His loved ones be.
To stand Himself in the midst of them,
   Though they count but two or three.

And forth we fared in the bitter rain.
   And our hearts had grown so warm,
It seemed like the pelting of summer flowers
   And not the crash of a storm;
" 'Twas a time of the dearest privilege
   At the Lord's right hand," we said,
And we thought how Jesus Himself had come
   To feed us the Living Bread.
             —MARGARET E. SANGSTER


## PRAYER

If you hear a prayer that moves you
   By its humble, pleading tone,
Join it—do not let the seeker
   Bow before his God alone.

*And let us consider one another, to provoke unto love and to good works: not forsaking the assembling of ourselves together.*
             —Heb. 10:24-25

Why should not your brother share
The strength of two or three in prayer?
—AUTHOR UNKNOWN

## SECRET SERVICE

If the "shut-ins" all united
    In one voice of common prayer—
What a ceaseless shower of blessing
    Would be falling everywhere!

Though so weak, and ofttimes helpless,
    They can wield a mighty power
Lifting up their soul's petition
    To the Saviour, hour by hour.

They can importune the Father,
    From the "secret place" and then—
In the quiet and the stillness
    They can hear Him speak to them.

Never soldier in fierce conflict
    Could a higher honor bring
Than the "shut-in," who's performing
    "Secret service" for the King.
—GERTRUDE ROBINSON DUGAN

# THE RESULTS OF PRAYER

*For every one that asketh receiveth; and he that seeketh findeth;
and to him that knocketh it shall be opened.*
—Matt. 7:8

More things are wrought by prayer
Than this world dreams of. Wherefore, let thy voice

*The effectual fervent prayer of a righteous man availeth much.*
—Jas. 5:16

Rise like a fountain for me night and day.
For what are men better than sheep or goats
That nourish a blind life within the brain,
If, knowing God, they lift not hands of prayer
Both for themselves and those who call them friend?
For so the whole round earth is every way
Bound by gold chains about the feet of God.

—ALFRED TENNYSON

## PRAYER

Prayer is the mightiest force that men can wield;
A power to which Omnipotence doth yield;
A privilege unparalleled, a way
Whereby the Almighty Father can display
His interest in His children's need and care.

Jehovah's storehouse is unlocked by prayer,
And faith doth turn the key.  Oh! would that men
Made full proof of this wondrous means, for then
Would mightier blessings on the Church be showered,
Her witness owned, her ministers empowered,
And souls ingathered.  Then the Gospel's sound
Would soon be heard to earth's remotest bound.
All things are possible if men but pray,
And if God did but limit to a day,
The time in which He'd note the upward glance,
Or fix the place, or name the circumstance,
When, where, or why petition could be brought,
Methinks His presence would by all be sought.

—AUTHOR UNKNOWN

## THE POWER OF PRAYER

There is an eye that never sleeps
Beneath the wing of night;

*Casting all your care upon him, for he careth for you.*  —I Pet. 5:7

There is an ear that never shuts
　　When sink the beams of light.
There is an arm that never tires
　　When human strength gives way;
There is a love that never fails.
That eye is fixed on seraph throngs;
That ear is filled with angels' songs;
That arm upholds the world on high;
That love is throned beyond the sky.
But there's a power which man can wield
　　When mortal aid is vain,
That eye, that arm, that love to reach,
　　That listening ear to gain;
That power is prayer, which soars on high,
And feeds on bliss beyond the sky.

—JOHN AIKMAN WALLACE

## PROOF

If radio's slim fingers
Can pluck a melody
From night, and toss it over
A continent or sea;

If the petaled white notes
Of a violin
Are blown across an ocean,
Or a city's din;

If songs, like crimson roses,
Are plucked from thin blue air,
Why should mortals wonder
If God hears prayer?

—ETHEL ROMIG FULLER

*It shall come to pass, that before they call, I will answer: and while
they are yet speaking, I will hear.*　　　　　—Isa. 65:24

## THIS I KNOW

I know not by what methods rare,
But this I know, God answers prayer.
I know that He has given His Word,
Which tells me prayer is always heard,
And will be answered, soon or late.
And so I pray and calmly wait.

I know not if the blessing sought
Will come in just the way I thought;
But leave my prayers with Him alone,
Whose will is wiser than my own,
Assured that He will grant my quest,
Or send some answer far more blest.

—ELIZA M. HICKOK

## ANSWERED PRAYER

God answers prayer; sometimes when hearts are weak
He gives the very gifts believers seek.
  But often faith must learn a deeper rest,
And trust God's silence when he does not speak;
  For, he whose name is Love will send the best.
Stars may burn out, nor mountain walls endure,
But God is true, his promises are sure
      To those who seek.

—MYRA GOODWIN PLANTZ

## I PRAYED TODAY

In my quiet room I talked with my Friend today;
I opened my heart to Him with its weight of care.
I spoke of the burdens I carried along the way;

*Thou shalt make thy prayer unto him, and he shall hear thee.*
—Job 22:27

217

I sought His help as I knelt at His feet in prayer.
I told Him my griefs, forgetting He knew them all;
I prayed for my own, forgetting that He could see
Within their hearts each need, though great or small,
Each unsolved problem and dark perplexity.

In my quiet room I talked with the Friend I love,
As He engineereed His planets, His stars, His suns;
My little world was what I was dreaming of,
My little day, and my own near precious ones.
And He with His hands on the universe, His eyes
Upon endless space and the sweep of eternity,
Bent above me, listening to my cries,
And, forgetting my faults and failures, answered me.
—Grace Noll Crowell

## SOMETIME, SOMEWHERE

Unanswered yet? the prayer your lips have pleaded
   In agony of heart these many years?
Does faith begin to fail?   Is hope departing?
   And think you all in vain those falling tears?
Say not the Father hath not heard your prayer;
You shall have your desire, sometime, somewhere.

Unanswered yet? though when you first presented
   This one petition at the Father's throne,
It seemed you could not wait the time of asking,
   So urgent was your heart to make it known.
Though years have passed since then, do not despair;
The Lord will answer you sometime, somewhere.

Unanswered yet? nay, do not say ungranted,
   ·Perhaps your part is not wholly done;

*Then shall ye call upon me, and ye shall go and pray unto me, and I*
*will hearken unto you.*        —Jer. 29:12

The work began when your first prayer was uttered,
   And God will finish what He has begun.
If you will keep the incense burning there,
His glory you shall see, sometime, somewhere.

Unanswered yet? Faith cannot be unanswered;
   Her feet are firmly planted on the rock,
Amid the wildest storms she stands undaunted,
   Nor quails before the loudest thunder shock.
She knows Omnipotence hath heard her prayer,
And cries, "It shall be done, sometime, somewhere."
              —OPHELIA G. BROWNING

## BLESSED

He prayed for strength that he might achieve;
He was made weak that he might obey.
He prayed for wealth that he might do greater things;
He was given infirmity that he might do better things,
He prayed for riches that he might be happy;
He was given poverty that he might be wise.
He prayed for power that he might have the praise of men;
He was given infirmity that he might feel the need of God.
He prayed for all things that he might enjoy life;
He was given life that he might enjoy all things.
He had received nothing that he asked for—all that he hoped for;
His prayer was answered—he was most blessed.
              —AUTHOR UNKNOWN

## LIGHT

It was so dark along my little street—
   Day's end had come without a lighted lamp,

*But seek ye first the kingdom of God, and his righteousness; and all*
*these things shall be added unto you.*       —Matt. 6:33

And I was lost as Israel's children were
 When they had toiled dim years in Egypt's camp.

I too, it seemed, had made bricks all the day
 That other hands might build a monument;
My vessel held no oil to break the dusk
 Of alien fields where I had pitched my tent.

Then suddenly I prayed—and there was light
 That left me warm and strangely unafraid;
When I am frightened now I always think
 Once it was dark and light came when I prayed.
       —HELEN WELSHIMER

## THE BULWARK OF HOME

Oh! precious, holy altar,
 Oh! sacred shrine of home,
Strength for the feet that falter,
 Light for the feet that roam!

'Tis here we seek the treasure
 God's Word so well reveals;
His love beyond all measure
 That blesses, cleanses, heals.

Here childish lips first murmur
 Sweet prayers to that dear Friend,
Here failing faith grows firmer
 As at God's throne we bend.

Yes, "They who seek shall find Me,"
 The promise never fails.

*And thou shalt teach them diligently unto thy children, and shalt talk of them when thou sittest in thine house, and when thou walkest by the way, and when thou liest down, and when thou risest up.*
       —Deut. 6:7

God's wings protect benignly
Homes where this Shrine prevails.
—GRACE B. PALMER

## PEACE

Within this humble thatched-roof place
Each meal is hallowed by a grace.

"Be present at our table, Lord,"
They pray around their frugal board.

"We thank Thee, Lord, for this our food;
God bless our home—and make us good."

Before they start each busy day
They meet around the hearth to pray.

At night beside the patchwork bed
"Our Father" is devoutly said.

The ancient Bible's leaves are loose
And shabby from continual use.

They're lowly peasants of the sod,
Yet all day long they walk with God.

Poor little home, and countrified,
But, oh, the peace one finds inside!
—BEATRICE PLUMB

## SOMEONE HAD PRAYED

The day was long, the burden I had borne
Seemed heavier than I could longer bear,

*If ye abide in me, and my words abide in you, ye shall ask what ye
will, and it shall be done unto you.* —John 15:7

And then it lifted, but I did not know
Someone had knelt in prayer,

Had taken me to God that very hour,
And asked the easing of the load, and He,
In infinite compassion, had stooped down
And taken it from me.

We can not tell how often as we pray
For some hurt one, bewildered and distressed,
The answer comes—but many times those hearts
Find sudden peace and rest.

Someone had prayed, and Faith, a reaching hand,
Took hold of God, and brought Him down that day!
So many, many hearts have need of prayer—
Oh, let us pray.

—GRACE NOLL CROWELL

## YOUR PRAYERS

When the battle is long, and I am weary with strife;
When the legions of sin and evil are rife;
I feel—and new courage flows into my life—
    That you are praying for me.

When victory comes out of seeming defeat,
And the dark lowering clouds shine with rainbows replete,
'Tis then that I know—and the assurance is sweet—
    That you are praying for me.

I'll gird tighter my armor and advance in the fight,
With a staunch heart and brave I'll battle for right,

*I thank my God upon every remembrance of you.*    —Phil. 1:3

I'll blench at no danger, and quail at no might—
   If you'll keep praying for me.

               —AUTHOR UNKNOWN


## THE SECRET

The weary one had rest, the sad had joy
   That day, and wondered how?
A ploughman singing at his work had prayed,
   "Lord, help them now."

Away in foreign lands they wondered how
   Their feeble words had power?
At home the Christians, two or three had met
   To pray an hour.

Yes, we are always wondering, wondering how,
   Because we do not see
Some one unknown perhaps, and far away,
   On bended knee.

               —AUTHOR UNKNOWN


## IN ALL THINGS, VICTORY

He hears me pray to Him upon the deep,
   When masts are gone, and tattered sails are blown
By storms that drive my frail boat out to sea;
   He hears, and sends the wind that wafts me home.

*Naught that can come shall bring despair to me,*
*Gaining in all things more than victory!*

He hears me pray to Him when I am lost
   Amid wild mountains, and no path can see;
He saves me from the beasts and from the night,
   And gives the comfort of His strength to me.

*The righteous cry, and the Lord heareth.*      —Ps. 34:17

He hears me pray to Him when my tired feet
　　Struggle across the desert's burning sand;
With His own blood restores my fainting soul,
　　And to green pastures leads me by the hand.
　　　　　　　　　　—Honami Nagata (a leper)
　　　　　　　　　　Trans. by Lois J. Erickson

## THE ANSWERED PRAYER
### Romans 8:26

I prayed for strength, and then I lost awhile
　　All sense of nearness, human and divine;
The love I leaned on failed and pierced my heart;
　　The hands I clung to loosed themselves from mine;
But while I swayed, weak, trembling, and alone,
The everlasting arms upheld my own.


I prayed for light; the sun went down in clouds,
　　The moon was darkened by a misty doubt,
The stars of heaven were dimmed by earthly fears,
　　And all my little candle flames burned out;
But while I sat in shadow, wrapped in night,
The face of Christ made all the darkness bright.


I prayed for peace, and dreamed of restful ease,
　　A slumber drugged from pain, a hushed repose;
Above my head the skies were black with storm,
　　And fiercer grew the onslaught of my foes;
But while the battle raged, and wild winds blew,
I heard His voice, and perfect peace I knew.

*For we know not what we should pray for as we ought: but the Spirit
itself maketh intercession for us.*　　　　　—Rom. 8:26

I thank Thee, Lord, Thou wert too wise to heed
   My feeble prayers, and answer as I sought,
Since these rich gifts Thy bounty has bestowed
   Have brought me more than I had asked or thought;
Giver of good, so answer each request
With Thine own giving, better than my best.

—ANNIE JOHNSON FLINT

# Acknowledgments and Indexes

# Acknowledgments

THANKS are due to the publishers and authors who have made possible this book by granting permission to include copyright poems:

## Publishers

Abingdon-Cokesbury Press for "The Secret" and "Too Busy?" from *Spiritual Hilltops*, and "The Parson's Prayer" from *Practicing the Presence* by Ralph S. Cushman; and for "Peace in Our Time, O Lord" by John Oxenham.

The Bobbs-Merrill Company for "The Prayer Perfect" from *Rhymes of Childhood* by James Whitcomb Riley, copyright, 1890, 1918.

Doubleday, Doran and Company, Inc., and A. P. Watt and Son for "Recessional" from *The Five Nations* by Rudyard Kipling, copyright, 1903, 1931.

E. P. Dutton and Company, Inc., copyright owner, for "House Blessing" from *Death and General Putnam & 101 Other Poems* by Arthur Guiterman.

Evangelical Publishers, Toronto, for "The Answered Prayer," "By the Way," "Our High Priest," "The Place of Prayer," "Prayer for a Friend," "The Sentinel," and "Thy Strength and My Day" by Annie Johnson Flint.

Harcourt, Brace and Company, Inc., for "Prayer for Courage" from *Selected Poems and Parodies of Louis Untermeyer*, and for "Father-Prayer" and "Mother-Prayer" from *The Old Road to Paradise* by Margaret Widdemer.

Harper and Brothers for "Someone Had Prayed" from *Light of the Years*, "A Prayer for Courage" and "Death" from *Songs for Courage*, and "I Prayed Today" from *Songs of Hope* by Grace Noll Crowell.

W. Heffer and Sons, Ltd., for "The Sacrament of Work" from *The Fourfold Sacrament* by J. S. Hoyland.

## ACKNOWLEDGMENTS

The Heidelberg Press for "Thy Word Is Like a Garden, Lord" by Edwin Hodder.

Houghton Mifflin Company for three stanzas of "A Prayer" by John Drinkwater.

The Hymn Society for "Prayer" by Henry Hallam Tweedy, copyright, 1929.

The Judson Press for "Lord, who lovest little children" by M. R., from *Childhood Songs;* and for "Our Thanks" by Nan F. Weeks.

*The King's Business* for poems by Luther B. Cross, A. J. Gordon, Annie S. Hawks, and Duncan McNeil.

Little, Brown and Company for "Prayer" from *Poems* by Helen Hunt Jackson.

The Macmillan Company for "Fulfil Thy Will" from *Poetical Works* by Christina G. Rossetti.

*The Moody Bible Institute Monthly* for poems by L. M. Hollingsworth and Walter J. Kuhn.

NEA Service, Inc., for "Light" by Helen Welshimer, copyrighted.

The Pilgrim Press for "The Extra Prayer" by Annie Willis McCullough from *Songs for Little People* by Danielson and Conant, "Now In the Days of Youth" by Walter J. Mathams from *Worship and Song,* and "Social Hymn for Children" from *As Children Worship* by Jeanette E. Perkins, all copyrighted.

The Presbyterian Board of Christian Education for "The Fellowship of Prayer" by Nancy Byrd Turner, copyright, 1928.

The Presbyterian Board of Foreign Missions for the Centennial Hymn, "God of Years, Thy Love Hath Led Us," by Jay Glover Eldridge, copyright, 1937.

Rand McNally and Company for "I Stretch My Thoughts" by Jeanette E. Perkins from *My Own Book of Prayers,* copyright, 1938, and "I'm Glad" by Elizabeth McE. Shields from *Prayers for Little Children,* copyright, 1936, both edited by Mary Alice Jones.

The Reilly and Lee Company for "A Prayer" from *Harbor Lights of Home* and "Lines for a Friend's House" from *Friends* by Edgar A. Guest. Copyrighted.

Fleming H. Revell Company for "Voyagers" from *Thy Sea Is Great, Our Boats Are Small* by Henry van Dyke, copyright, 1922.

The Rodeheaver Hall-Mack Company for "An Evening Prayer" by C. Maude Battersby, copyright, 1911, by Chas. H. Gabriel, Homer

A. Rodeheaver, owner; "From Dawn to Evensong" by C. Austin Miles, copyright, 1937, by The Rodeheaver Company; and "In Remembrance" by Julia Benson Parker, copyright, 1936, by Homer A. Rodeheaver.

Round Table Press for "A Mother Speaks" from *All Through the Day* by Margaret E. Sangster.

Charles Scribner's Sons, Inc., for "Bedtime Prayer," "Night-Watch Prayer," and "Prayer" by Henry van Dyke, and poems by Maltbie D. Babcock and Sidney Lanier.

*The Sunday School Times* for "A Christmas Song" by Ruth Winant Wheeler, and poems by Opal Leonore Gibbs, Philip E. Howard, Edith M. Lee, and Edith L. Mapes.

## Authors

Charles Carroll Albertson for "Prayer at a Wedding" from *Prayers and Reflections of a Modern Disciple,* Samuel Bagster and Sons, London, publishers.

Irene Arnold for "Pray!"

Claribel Weeks Avery for "Vespers."

Marie Barton for "Home of My Thoughts," "New Year," "Peace on Earth," "Thanksgiving Day," and "What Is Prayer?"

Ruby Dell Baugher for "A Christmas Prayer."

J. M. Bemiss for "A Minister's Prayer."

Chester K. Bolton for "Faith" by his mother, Sarah K. Bolton.

Florence Bone for "Prayer for a Little Home."

Mouzon W. Brabham for "A Father's Prayer."

William Stanley Braithwaite for "A Sea-Prayer."

Mrs. L. D. Burkhalter, Jr., for "This I Know" by her grandmother, Eliza M. Hickok.

Lucy Carruth for "My Prayer."

Mazie V. Caruthers for "Prayer of a Tired Woman."

Thomas Curtis Clark for "Unto Thee."

Robert J. Craig for "Evening."

Grace Noll Crowell for the Foreword, written especially for this book.

Arthur B. Dale for "Sound Thy Trumpet, God of Action."

Chester M. Davis for "An Easter Prayer."

ACKNOWLEDGMENTS

Margaret Deland for "Doubt."

Gertrude Robinson Dugan for "Our Airmen" and "Secret Service."

Lois J. Erickson for her translations of two poems by Honami Nagata from *Hearts Aglow*.

John Finley for "Matins."

Alice Reynolds Flower for "At All Times."

Alexander Louis Fraser for "Rallying Hymn for the Church."

The late Robert Freeman for "Evening Prayer" and "God Bless Our Home."

Ethel Romig Fuller for "Proof."

Opal Leonore Gibbs for "Interceding."

Samuel McP. Glasgow (Green Forest) for "Not My Will."

James M. Gray for the last stanza of "Pray One for Another."

Daniel Henderson for "Hymn for a Household."

Mary T. Higginson for "The Things I Miss" by her husband, Thomas Wentworth Higginson.

Leslie Pinckney Hill for "The Teacher."

L. M. Hollingsworth for "Intercession."

George Klingle Holmes for "Make Thy Way Mine."

Mrs. Mary E. Hoskinson for "The Fault Is Mine" by her daughter, Mrs. Edith M. Lee.

Philip E. Howard, Jr., for "Strength in Weakness" by his father.

Oliver Huckel for "Unanswered Prayer."

Mrs. Robert F. Jefferys for "Dedication" by her father, Louis F. Benson.

Alice B. Joynes for "For Those Who Fly."

Samuel E. Kiser for "A Little Prayer."

Grenville Kleiser for "My Daily Prayer," "Our Refuge and Strength," "Prayer," and "We Thank Thee."

Edgar Daniel Kramer for "New Year Prayer."

Walter J. Kuhn for "My Only Plea."

R. A. Lapsley, Jr., for "Psalm Fifty-One" written by his father.

The late Calvin W. Laufer for "Evening Prayer," "Morning Prayer," and "A Prayer Poem." Copyright by the author.

J. Shenton Lodge for "Prayer for Any Bride and Groom."

William Ludlum for "Let Us Come Before His Presence," "The Stairway to the Stars," and "Thanksgiving."

Christie Lund for "Prayer for a Bride's House."

Lois Givens Vaughan McLain for "An Aged Couple Gives Thanks" and "Thanksgiving for Benefits Received."

Edith L. Mapes for "Shall I Pray On?"

Virgil Markham for "A Prayer" by his father, Edwin Markham.

Dwight Edwards Marvin for "Lord, Give Me Faith," "Nearing the Ford," "Sabbath Morning Worship," "Sleeplessness," and "Vesper Bells."

Whitney Montgomery for "Revelation" and "Thanksgiving."

Joseph Morris for "A Prayer for Courage" from *Facing Forward,* copyright, 1925. A. L. Burt Company, publishers.

Anna Norman Oates for "Thy Will Be Done."

The late John Oxenham for "A Prayer for Peace," "Spread the Light," and two poems entitled "A Prayer."

Grace B. Palmer for "The Bulwark of Home."

Julia Benson Parker for "The Perfect Gift."

The late W. T. Pearman for "Prayer."

Beatrice Plumb for "Peace."

Dorothy Dix Porges for "Tell It To God."

Norman E. Richardson for "A Prayer for Aviators" and "The Teacher's Prayer," copyrighted.

Ella Broadus Robertson for "Prayer for a College Girl."

Lexie Dean Robertson for "Radio Prayer."

Margaret E. Sangster for "In Gratitude for Friends" (written especially for this book), "Gratitude," "A Mother Speaks," "Our Missionaries," and "At Prayer Meeting."

Alice E. Sherwood for "A Hymn of Thanksgiving" and "Into a Mountain Apart."

Elizabeth McE. Shields for "God Is Near" from *Worship and Conduct Songs,* and "The Prayer of a Teacher."

Agnes Smyth Kelsey Shute for "Our Father, As We Start the Day."

William L. Stidger for a couplet from "A Child's Prayer."

Ethel Arnold Tilden for "Dedication."

Ruby Weyburn Tobias for "Prayer Time."

## ACKNOWLEDGMENTS

John F. Todd for "A Prayer for Mothers."

Grace E. Troy for "A Pastor's Prayer" and "A Pastor's Prayer for His Congregation."

Nancy Byrd Turner for "Christmas," "Easter Prayer," "A Prayer," "A Prayer at Christmas Time," "Prayer on Christmas Eve," "Prayer at New Year's," "Prayer at Thanksgiving Time," and "The Teacher's Prayer."

Mary Hoge Wardlaw for "Easter."

Nan F. Weeks for "Our Thanks."

Anna M. Wells for "The People's Prayer," "Pray!" "Pray For Me," "Prayer for the President," and "The Prayer Meeting," all by her husband, Amos R. Wells.

Helen Welshimer for "Light," copyrighted by NEA Service, Inc., and "Prayer for a Bride."

Ruth Winant Wheeler for "A Christmas Song" and "A Nurse's Prayer."

B. Y. Williams for "A Prayer" from *House of Happiness*.

Harriet B. Williams for "Guidance."

George W. Wiseman for "Youth's Prayer."

Bertha Gerneaux Woods for "At His Table," "Dedication of a Home," "Open My Eyes," "Prayer for Faith in Peace," and "Prayer on Entering Church."

# Index of Subjects

# Index of Authors

# Index of Titles

# Index of First Lines